Elizabeth Sk

Can I Talk to You?

**How to be a counselor,
parent or friend
of teenagers**

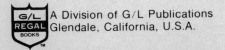

A Division of G/L Publications
Glendale, California, U.S.A.

Copyright © 1977 by G/L Publications. Originally
published by Inter-Varsity Christian Fellowship of
the United States of America. This 1977 edition
published by G/L Publications with permission of
Inter-Varsity Press and the author. All rights
reserved.

Published by
Regal Books Division, G/L Publications
Glendale, California 91209,
Printed in U.S.A.

Library of Congress Catalog Card Number applied for
ISBN 0-8307-0557-0

In memorium to
Dr. E. Boyd Shannon
whose advice at Pasadena College
(now Point Loma)
encouraged me to pursue
a career in counseling.

Contents

Foreword

I read this book with great pleasure. Over the years that Elizabeth Skoglund has been consulting me concerning her work with students and their problems I have watched her natural talents along these lines become honed into the sharp skills of a good licensed psychotherapist. Her approach in this book is internally consistent and psychologically valid. Miss Skoglund combines a natural warmth and empathy with a sophisticated understanding of human behavior. This combination reveals itself throughout this book. She has made a valuable contribution in a much-needed area.

This sensitive, human approach is sometimes not apparent in the current deluge of publications concerning teenagers' problems. It should be helpful to teachers, parents and others who feel some personal interest or responsibility for these salvageable youth who with desperate futility attempt to establish a successful identity by various detrimental means. I have been pleased and complimented to be given the opportunity to recommend the book. I do so without reservation.

Glenn K. Wiest
Associate
Institute for Reality Therapy
Los Angeles, California

Preface

After my first three years of teaching high school English, I became uncomfortably aware that, while the teaching of academic subjects would always hold a certain fascination for me, I was becoming increasingly interested in counseling. At that time I had the good fortune to sign up for a counseling course at Pasadena College, taught by the late Dr. E. Boyd Shannon under whose advice I was encouraged to further my training. As I progressed from student to counselor, my best training and practical advice came from Glenn K. Wiest, Clinical Psychologist, Institute for Reality Therapy. To him I am indebted for time and interest which are beyond my ability to repay.

During the years in working with hundreds of students—first in a school setting and then in the privacy of a counseling office—I have become aware of the need for a book relating to teenagers, a book that emphasizes a blending of good psychological principles and Christian beliefs. Whether we counsel in the capacity of parent, teacher, counselor, Sunday School teacher, pastor or just interested friend, there are many opportunities and indeed the necessity for helping troubled teenagers. Yet the world of the teenager is a never-never land, often obscure and strange to the adult world. *Can I Talk to You?* is intended to penetrate that world and report with clarity and practicality the how-to of working with and understanding and counseling teenagers.

While it is hoped that this book will help some in the counseling field, the primary thrust is to aid the layman who lives with teenage problems rather than the professional who can walk away and forget it. Parents, in particular, who have often taken on an unfair measure of guilt over the problems of their children will hopefully benefit and receive positive encouragement.

Elizabeth Skoglund
Burbank, California
July 1977

chapter one

The Dilemma of the Modern Teenager

A ring of the phone one evening interrupted my work. At first I failed to recognize my caller. Then I picked up telltale clues—varying moods, sullen hostility, pathetic helplessness. It was Linda Barclay.

"Oh, God!" she blurted into the receiver. "I'm going to a party to get loaded and you can't stop me! I can't stay in this house one more minute. Muriel and I are going to find a bunch of parties." And then more quietly, "I don't want to go, but I can't stay here. All they do is put me down and yell at each other."

Rather hesitantly, I invited her to spend the evening with me and a friend. The instant enthusiasm in her voice convinced me that I had done the right thing.

On our way to pick up Linda, I thought back over the trauma of her life during the past several weeks. She seemed withdrawn and aloof in my classes. Then one day she came to school so stoned on acid and alcohol that a boy friend had to half carry her to her seat. I took her to another room and quickly called for the nurse and her parents.

As we waited for her mother to come, Linda sat hunched up, her long, dark hair covering her face most of the time. She rocked back and forth, attempting periodically to hit her head against the wall. She punctuated her physical gyrations with wild cries and obscenities, sometimes begging, "Just let me die!" She kept asking for cigarettes and pleaded with me not to send her home.

"My father'll kill me. They don't care about me. They never have."

I knew that her father had beaten her brother so viciously that the youngster had run away from home.

Now as my friend and I approached Linda's house, I was apprehensive. How would we be received? Was it all a mistake?

The house was new, lovely, beautifully landscaped. The pleasant, rather pretty woman who met us at the door was soon joined by her husband, a successful architect. He too looked like a normal, civilized parent.

The mother began to talk of her concern for Linda. She was tense and near tears as she spoke of her need for help in coping with their problem. The father also said he wanted to help. By then they had at last faced the fact that their daughter was on drugs and alcohol, but they could not tell when she was using them. I was amazed at their apparent ignorance of what was going on with Linda. It seemed they actually preferred it that way. The mother told me, "Please help Linda, but don't tell us exactly what she's doing. We'd rather not know."

The parents admitted faults, such as over-drinking, quick tempers and an assortment of frustrations. And what they said showed they were regrettably united in their utter inability to understand a daughter whom they said they loved.

At that point, Linda entered the room with an angry expression on her face. There was an embarrassed silence, and then Linda said abruptly, "Let's go. I'll be home later." Her parents assented and casually saw us to the door. Both the parents and Linda were indifferent and awkward in each other's presence.

I have come to know Linda well in the months that have elapsed since that night at her house. We have talked for hours—sometimes on the phone, sometimes in my family counseling office. We have discussed her feelings about life—that it is all pain with almost no happiness apart from alcohol and drugs, that life and people alike are warped—and her conviction that she can never make it. I have agonized with her in her effort to "put down" getting high on chemicals and in her failure to ever really do so. I have felt momentary flickers of elation when she seemed to be gaining some strength, but more often, I have listened to her resignation to a life of addiction. She cannot believe she could ever be a part of what she calls "your world of reality." Her reality has been jail, excessive and increasingly dangerous experimentation with chemicals and blackouts.

I wonder where it will all end. What are the chances she can still be reached? Will she even live long enough for someone to stay close enough to her to really help? I know that for a while we were close, but that closeness was too threatening to her because I represented hope. If you hope, you can be hurt and disappointed. She cannot stand that. Will I pick up the paper some day and read that she has overdosed? Or will I hear that she has been killed in violence of some kind? Will I find out only afterward that she has committed suicide.

Why Do We Become Strangers?

Why do so many young people become so estranged from our adult world that we can hardly reach them even when we want to? Why must two normal, respectable parents live as utter strangers with the children they brought into the world? Why does each persist in playing a role, all the while feeling alone, afraid, rejected? How can they be inhabitants of the same house, part of each other—but, in the truest sense of the word, be strangers?

Even those recently out of high school—college freshmen and older—seem to have shut down the lines of communication between themselves and the teenage population. As a 19-year-old graduate said to me at a high school football game, "I feel old. It all seems so different."

This is a curious phenomenon since many of the problems which exist on the high school campus certainly continue into college—problems of alienation, striving to find oneself and the resultant symptoms of drug abuse, alcoholism, misuse of sex and interest in the occult. Yet, somehow each age group isolates itself from the other. The result is that many teenagers do not feel any more understood by their older brothers and sisters than by their parents. And many young people in their early twenties become annoyed with what they cannot understand in friends who are a few years younger.

Then, too, how many teachers completely fail to understand a student struggling daily to communicate his frustrations? How many ministers are totally baffled when their young people drop out of church, and are at a loss to figure out how to rekindle their interest? How many policemen feel more comfortable handling a hardened criminal than a young "incorrigible"? How many mothers are afraid to ask "the girl next door" to baby-sit

14

for fear something will happen while they are gone?

Most adults wonder what in the world is going on with youngsters these days, while teenagers have equal doubts about the behavior of the older generation. The result is a communication gap, and contrary to the belief of most adults, today's youth see it, try to understand it and even try to look at both sides of the problem.

"The most important thing of all," said one of my students, "is a good father-son relationship. This is one thing I don't have now and wish I had. I try to look at this disadvantage in an objective way. I figure that my father has brought too many obligations onto himself and he's trapped, so I just go along for the ride. But when he does get time off, he just goes and does what he enjoys and doesn't pay any attention to me or the rest of the family. Maybe I'm being a little hard on him, because, after all, he's getting on in life and looking forward to retirement."

Adults may be able to get along well without children, but their children need them. Young people wish they could communicate across the gap. Often they express their desire almost wistfully.

One drug user, who feels that she cannot talk to her parents at all, showed her father a copy of Art Linkletter's moving, penetrating letter to his daughter which deals with the whole idea of the generation gap. Shari was trying to communicate her own deep feelings to her father by showing it to him. He missed the clue entirely and brushed the whole incident aside with the comment that it was "nice."

The generation gap has been talked about and argued over until it is a topic which people would prefer to avoid altogether. Yet this gap, which has existed between all generations down through history, has widespread implications for this generation.

Struggling with Twentieth-Century Shock

Walter Lippmann stated, "Our ancestors thought they knew their way from birth to eternity; we are puzzled about the day after tomorrow."[1] This is precisely the dilemma of the modern teenager. The world around him is undergoing constant upheaval. He must face adult realities before he has had time to enjoy the unburdened years of childhood. He is inundated with first-hand information on wars, power struggles, riots, and assassinations. He knows about the devastations of earthquakes, epidemics, exploitation, and pollution. And he fears he will not live to adulthood. No one seems to need the teenagers of this generation in this over-populated world—not, at least, until they are old enough to fight or vote. Thus our teens feel peculiarly alone, isolated and alienated.

One of my students, a 15-year-old boy, summed up his feelings: "I am a lost person, searching for who I am. I'm mixed into a world of hate, a world in which I don't think I belong. Depressed, lost, searching, not liking what I see. Who am I? I don't really know for sure. I guess I'm just lost."

Stressing the same idea, a girl wrote: "Right now I'm very confused with life. I feel there is nothing in it. I don't know whether I should commit suicide or keep struggling to be someone, something in the maze of growing up."

A boy echoed her doubts with this desperate query, "What is life all about? Is it a big game? Who are the winners and losers? And if life is so depressing, why not kill yourself?"

Another youth put his thoughts into verse:

They pollute our seas,
They pollute our land,

They pollute our air
and where am I?

They pollute our birds,
They pollute our plants,
They pollute our minds
and where am I?

The teenage years are a natural time for students to ask such questions about the real meaning of life. Granted, the questions they ask are not easy. But when adults placate or give only superficial or materialistic answers, it is not surprising that young people feel hostile and further alienated f om an adult world that seems unable to even understand their questions.

To be sure, adults have problems of their own. Walter Lippmann has appropriately said that "No mariner ever enters upon a more uncharted sea than does the average human being born in the twentieth century."[2] We are all suffering from the confusion of the fast pace of life, the frustrations of social and moral change, and the frightening challenges of modern technology.

What other generation has had to worry about a population explosion that could lead to government controls over family size? What other generation has ever traveled hundreds of miles an hour to a two-hour business appointment? How many people prior to this century have known within twenty-four hours the casualty list from a war thousands of miles away?

Too often the young person finds that the adult world he turns to still has not yet found its own meaning or answered its own questions. But where else can a teenager get help?

One girl expressed her pent-up frustration in this poem:

I talk to the walls
To get the answers
To the questions that I ask.
My questions are hard,
They are all about life—

We are born for a purpose,
A purpose on this earth.
Here's another question
I feel I should ask,
What was the purpose of *my* birth?

What's the purpose
Of my foolish tale?
Life's a boat,
I've lost the sail.

The Plea for Help

In their search for themselves and their place in this world, today's teenagers need guidance perhaps more than any other generation because there are more options available today. Educational opportunities alone are greater than they have ever been and are more available to the poor as well as the rich. A wide variety of choices exists in the area of philosophical-religious beliefs. Furthermore, the depersonalization of life as cities grow in population leaves people free to make more private, individual decisions about how they conduct their lives. Thus, there is a greater need for guidance. But that help is not always forthcoming and young people are often forced to make decisions without the support and direction they really need.

Because there are more options available today, there are alarmingly greater possibilities for self-destructive choices. Whenever a person looks for answers, there are negative as well as positive possibilities. We need only look around us to see the destructive potential of having to make choices.

Morally, for example, many teenagers today do not consider premarital sex wrong. Now that the pill and the availability of abortions have removed the threat of pregnancy, one of the strongest arguments young people have been given against premarital sex has also been removed. This combined with little or no emphasis on sin and minimal understanding of the psychological problems inherent in free love, has left many teenagers rudderless in a sea of confusion.

"Right now," said a teen, "because of my age and experience, I feel that deciding whether to accept sex when it comes along or to put it down is one of my most difficult tasks. I want it, but I'm afraid of being sorry afterwards. Don't get me wrong—I wouldn't just do it with anyone. It would have to be the guy I'm in love with. But still, I'm kind of at war with myself. . . ."

The idea that it might be wrong even when one is in love frequently does not enter the picture. Indeed, the idea of sexual experience under conditions of love or as a trial of compatibility for marriage is often considered moral and right. Having no strong religious convictions about marriage, many young people question the whole institution of marriage in a society where it is not too successful.

In working out their own solutions, young people sometimes slip into an idealism which is misguided and contradictory. During the Vietnam war, a large percentage of one of my classes expressed an intense desire for world peace and love for all mankind. Yet the next day, when I was absent, the class gave my substitute a rough time. When I came back and read the note from the substitute, I confronted the class with their inconsistency. Their desire for love and peace in Vietnam was phony if in their school they were unable to show consideration for another human being.

We had a rather heated discussion for about forty-five minutes; both sides were free to speak openly. It is to their credit that my students were able to see and admit their inconsistency. But they did not see this inconsistency on their own; it had to be pointed out to them.

Today's young people are a subculture which tends to respond passively in some situations while in other instances they become aroused to violence. They are not about to watch an increasingly complex and depersonalized society crush them; if need be, they will defy the system that ignores them. One young boy related his discontent with school to me and in many ways his complaints seemed justified. When I told him that he could improve conditions by legal means as well as rioting, he agreed, but added, "It will take 10 years your way while my way would take one day." That rationale for rebellion is hard to argue against yet the solution would be simple enough if the adult world would only listen. And unfortunately, when activist rebellion does not achieve their ends, most of these young people slip into a passive, self-centered indifference. That, too, is sad and would sometimes be avoided if we adults would at least hear their side of the story.

What Teenagers Want from Adults

The so-called "establishment" is usually enraged at the teenager's individualism and defiance of authority. It does not bother to sort out the unfulfilled needs which necessitate violence or passivity. It totally misses the feelings of helplessness and inadequacy which frequently motivate the actions of young people. Instead of listening when the complaints and questions first start, the

20

establishment too often ignores passivity and waits for overt rebellion and then wonders why neither side can be rational enough to understand the other. In overreaction to rebellion, adult power can give the young person the lifelong stigma of a jail sentence.

All the while teenagers are rebelling against the adult world, they are really begging it to help them. Not that they want ideas forced on them, but they do want guidance wherein they are still ultimately free to choose their own way.

Their need is to be needed by someone or something. They have plenty of *things*, but what they want is the kind of love which says, "I care. I am not afraid of you. I need you. I like you as you are." Without this love, they feel a lack of worth. For it is impossible to feel worthwhile if you suspect that no one really cares about you, that no one would miss you if you just disappeared, that, in fact, you know people would just as soon be rid of you.

One girl told me that all of her life her parents have given her money to go to a show, go shopping or spend the day at the beach. She says, "They just want to get me out of the way." Mistaken or not, her interpretation of her parents' "generosity" is that she is not worth having around.

Tom is a 16-year-old boy whose mother recently remarried. To say the least, Tom is not overly fond of his new "father." Rather than take time to help Tom adjust to the new home situation, his mother bought him an expensive motorcycle and ignored the problem. Tom loves his cycle, but he still hates his stepfather. People who do not know him say he is spoiled because he has a car, a motorcycle and plenty of spending money. Actually he is deprived because he lacks the warm family relationship he desires and needs.

21

Because youth today are surrounded by material things, these things sometimes mean little. And since much of the competition and ambition of the adult world is aimed at earning large amounts of money which will in turn buy a comfortable, plush life, many young people who scorn materialism also avoid the education and job which buy that materialism. Yet, interestingly enough, these same young people rebel when they begin to suffer too intensely from lack of things.

A boy who transferred to our school in the middle of his junior year began to get low grades and seemed to have no motivation whatever. One day when I asked him about his school work, his answer was blunt: "Why should I study? If I do, I'll just get better grades and get into a good college. Then, eventually, I'll have a well-paying job, nice home, two cars instead of one. When I die, I'll just leave it all to my children and they'll go through the same cycle." Understandably, the materialistic rat race does not offer him rewards appealing enough for all the work he would have to put into it.

For this and similar reasons, many repudiate the material and "drop out" into the simple life of the commune or the mind-expanding world of drugs in their desperate search to find purpose and meaning.

How the Church Alienates Its Teens

Perhaps the most difficult search of all is the quest for spiritual meaning in life. A girl whose parents abandoned her when she was about fourteen asks this poignant question:

> As we live day by day
>   and life goes on,
> People dance merrily through
>   the days without a care.

22

But even though I can't place
   all reasons for problems,
Sometimes I wonder
   why I should have them now.
Is God alive?
   If He is, is He deaf?
He doesn't hear the cry of need.
Why should I keep calling?

Yet, young people who are looking for God do not always find Him when they go to church. In fact the organized church tends to turn many teenagers off.

A small group of teenagers sat in my office one day discussing problems which affected them. One of them made a disparaging remark about churches. All unanimously supported him. Churches, they said, were filled with cliques—cliques full of gossips who made it their business to find out all the bad things which could be unearthed about a person.

One boy, whom the last time I heard had turned to heroin, said he liked to go to church when no one else was there, for then he could try to find God. Once again the group agreed. Church seemed irrelevant to them, but God was someone they wanted to know.

One teenager aptly expressed the feelings of the others, "Churches are too bogged down in ritual and aren't very strong in the God loves you department. They don't tell it like it is when it comes to God. They teach us to love thy neighbor as thyself and then when someone walks into church with long hair they condemn him and say, we don't want you to be part of our little group. Get lost. It's no wonder kids find it so hard to believe."

Another girl said, "They complain about our casual clothes and about how wild we are. They don't have any right to say anything about these things because we are all there for the same reason—to learn about God."

Furthermore, many of these young people seemed to feel that there is little spiritual substance in many churches—just social life. Unfortunately, I could not entirely disagree with them since in my own experience with churches I have found that many times the focus is on meetings, new buildings, "innovative" programs and almost anything but the reality of Christ. One time when I was teaching a junior high Sunday School class in a small church, the church itself was going through a crisis. Numbers were decreasing and the young people were not coming. The church leaders decided to rebuild and modernize the *building* in order to "attract" the young people! Today that church has its building but it still has not solved its problem. It has almost no outreach to young people and little even to the surrounding adult community.

The Challenge for Parents, Teachers and Church Leaders

The home, the educational institution and the church all face one of the greatest challenges ever. They cannot substitute things, gimmicks and outright lies for relevancy and reality. Nor can they continue to deny and ignore the needs of today's teenagers. Although many teenagers of this generation are unreached by the established institutions of our society, they are not at all unreachable. These teens question our values, but they seek concrete reasons for life. They rebel, but they want guidance. They act sure of themselves and independent of society, but they feel alone. The haunting words of one 16-year-old boy point out the path we must chart for today's youth:

"I am a person who has no personal philosophy of his

24

own. I feel like a small boat caught in the current of a large river being carried in the mainstream of life toward an unknown destination. But what is ahead, what is life, success? They all are abstract, comparative terms. Keeping up with the Joneses isn't half as hard as being the Joneses. What is success? One day I'll inherit a business. What will I have to work for then? Sure, my dad wants me to have everything he didn't have—and understandably so. But when everything is said and done, what does money buy besides fine cars, a yacht, a ten-room house on a hill with a pool? Where do you go to buy happiness?"

We cannot tell our troubled teens where to go to "buy" happiness, but we can and must guide them through these tempestuous years of development toward self-discovery and a deeper maturity of body, mind and spirit.

In Summary

1. The teenager in today's world feels peculiarly alone and confused about his role in life.

2. While he may seem to resist adult interference on the one hand, he has a deep craving for an adult who will listen and really hear him; someone to understand his feelings and be willing to get involved in his life.

3. The spiritual potential of the teenage years is often underestimated. Teenagers need a personal, real relationship with God. Their sincere seeking needs to be taken seriously, spiritual guidance provided and Christian growth nurtured.

chapter two

The Drug Culture:
A Temporary Escape

One afternoon Bruce drank a few beers and took a couple of very mild pills (aspirin and Librium). Later in the day he took his girl friend Sue to a park where they both smoked a joint. Then rather suddenly Bruce started to trip out.

He saw his girl friend become a strange, grotesque creature, distorted and ugly. Slowly he began to panic. He was even afraid of Sue! "Help me!" he pleaded with her, while at the same time he warned her to "stay away."

Sue was thoroughly confused. At first she did not believe Bruce. After all, who trips out after one joint? And who trips out from marijuana anyway? Yet there he was, claiming to be hallucinating. "Come on, stop putting me on," she said. And then, "I'm frightened, maybe we should get help."

After about four days of alternating between feelings of near normalcy and near insanity, Bruce called me because a friend had said I might be able to help.

Actually there was little I could do. I was not even

sure what was wrong. I, too, could not believe that it was just the marijuana. I suspected LSD or STP and wondered if some "Angel Dust," an animal tranquilizer, had been added.

In a practical sense the first step was to get Bruce with a responsible person for the night. Since he lived with his alcoholic father who was drunk at the time, there was no help from that source. His mother might have cared, but she had remarried and was living in another state. Realizing that no one even suspected of being on LSD should be left alone, we arranged for him to spend the night at the home of one of his friends whose parents understood the problem and were willing to help. With the help of several friends we got him to a clinic the next day.

Interestingly, the doctors at the clinic concluded that the marijuana, possibly with "Angel Dust" added, and the combination of alcohol and pills he had taken earlier had provided a catalyst which triggered off some bad psychological reactions.

Bruce had all the problems which so many students have who start on drugs: an insecure home, a poor self-image and a sense of purposelessness in life. Drugs are not the real problem; they just cover it up for a while and, of course, add a new problem to the list.

Sue, who had taken almost everything Bruce had taken, did not experience any adverse side effects. But weeks later, with different psychological stresses, she also had bad reactions to drugs.

The Drug Scene Today

Sue and Bruce are just two young people who represent a substantial segment of today's teenagers. The drug scene has broadened from a former emphasis on hard drugs to more socially acceptable drugs—pills,

LSD and mainly alcohol and marijuana. In the past, drug abuse was generally limited to the ghetto-criminal types and alcoholism was almost unknown among teenagers. The drug user was a lowly-regarded minority in the typical school of yesterday. Today, almost all students are openly and continually exposed to drug and alcohol abuse. The cheerleader, the football hero and the straight-A student are as much a part of the scene as the delinquent and the criminal. Conventional hair styles and dress guarantee nothing in the realm of drug experimentation.

Many teenagers who go to drug parties off campus are pretty average-looking. They go to school regularly, take out the trash and wash the dishes at home and may even go to church on Sunday. Any young person on almost any campus in this country can have access to any drug he desires with little exercise of his own ingenuity.

Among teenagers, a chemical high has become so important that it pervades much of their social life. It has become next to impossible for any teenager to avoid contact with alcohol and drugs. Most teenagers are at least offered some form of illegal drug.

In talking to a friend recently I was intrigued as he told me of their move to a small town in hopes that they could avoid exposure of their young children to illegal drugs. The town's population totaled 50 people and the population of the nearest large town reached only 1,000 people. Said he, "Every kid in this town has immediate access to marijuana." And, worse still, the quantities sold are large because law enforcement is minimal in such a small town.

Wherever they live, those teenagers who do resist are nevertheless hurt and confused because close friends become entangled with the drug culture. Where does

29

their loyalty lie? When do they turn someone in? What can they do when they find classmates hurting themselves?

One girl states this latter problem well: "I grew up with a girl that has really been close to me. I went through sixth grade having her as my best friend. Then in seventh grade I moved down here. We goofed around for a long time off and on until I didn't hear from her any more. I went up to her house one day and she was *so* ripped, she was *so* loaded on acid, she didn't even know who I was. I stayed with her that day and that night until finally she crashed and slept the rest of the night. I stayed up just watching her sleep wondering what had happened, who and what had started her like this. I was just in shock seeing her like this. And why her, my friend. I didn't know the least thing about how to tell her she was doing the wrong thing, taking life wrong, going the wrong way. She woke up and didn't know a thing that had happened the night before.

"When she was still asleep I was looking around her room for anything I could find. I looked in a drawer and I just about died. There was a bunch of reds, joints, acid and junk. I took them and flushed them down the toilet. She scared me to death because I didn't know what I should do, tell her mom, keep it to myself, tell my mom, I didn't know.

"When she woke up, she knew me and started crying for me not to tell her mom. I promised her I wouldn't and I still haven't. Maybe she started because her dad had died, but I don't think so because he died when she was in 4th grade. I just don't know. She isn't happy, she hates life and herself, hates her mom, but yet she keeps drugs up.

"To me, after staying with her that night, and all the hours I've spent with her when she was so loaded she couldn't even talk, I don't think dope is the answer. She calls me up loaded out of her mind and says she *thinks* she is having fun. I've been with her when she has tried to slash her wrists but I stopped the bleeding, I just think she's sick. Still with all of this and her and me the exact opposite, I still love her as my own sister, that's what I can't understand. I've been so mad at her different times but I still love her. I guess I do because I remember her how she was and only when I see her, I remember her the way she is now.

"I can just feel some day that I will go up to see her, go in her room and she will be dead. I guess it can't help but I still pray for her, that she will stop drugs, but I can't help by praying. She finally will stop drugs when she's dead."

Pot Parties and Alcoholism

A great many young people who do not use pills as such are confronted by the confusion of whether to drink alcohol or smoke marijuana. Even that would not be so great a problem except that almost all teenage parties rely heavily on both pot and booze for entertainment. And many teenagers end up at parties or social gatherings where drugs are used.

One girl describes a pot party this way: "One evening two girls and four guys decided to have a party, so everyone brought booze and the mix for the drinks. Everyone got up and started to dance, drink and crack jokes. After a while the guys started to roll the joints. They picked through it to get the best pieces for their joint. After they finished rolling the pot, they began to smoke it, but the smell got so bad that the two girls had to go out and get some fresh air. When they finished they sat down and figured out that between the four of them they had rolled and smoked ten joints. That night was the first time one of the boys had ever smoked one, so when the joints would come around to him and he would take a drag his face would turn bright red. It took the guys until the next morning to come down because they had smoked so many joints and drunk quite a lot of alcohol."

Another describes the end of a party: "Usually they leave all stoned and happy and I can see that they had a good time."

The milder parties may be limited to drinking and smoking pot. Those not so mild may involve LSD and even heroin. Sex becomes a by-product of the lowering of inhibitions through drugs.

One boy described a typical party at his house: "There was nobody but me and all my friends. My people were gone all weekend. That house stunk like you name it when the party was over. There were couples sleeping all over the house, in the bathtub, closet— everybody was so drunk and stoned."

A more subtle way in which young people are confronted with drugs is in a social situation where parents either approve of or ignore what is happening. One middle-class mother and dad simply go upstairs and allow their son to smoke grass with his friends downstairs. The son and his friends think his parents are really with it. They laugh about other adults who go to pieces if they find a "lid" in their teenager's room, but who are relieved or indifferent to find only empty whiskey bottles. They feel they have as much right to use drugs as their mothers have to use diet pills and tranquilizers and their right to drink is as legitimate as that of their fathers who stay after work and have a few drinks with the guys.

When the average teacher sees these light drug users, their facade of normalcy has been resumed. These students go to class, contribute to discussions, take tests.

They may have taken a few uppers on the way to school. They may smoke a little grass in the washroom during lunch. Some may mix vodka with their cokes at lunchtime, while their teachers, often good teachers, say things like: "I've never had anyone stoned in my classroom" or "Joe is such a nice boy, but I don't know why he doesn't study. He's got such potential, but he's wasting it because he's so lazy."

Reasons for Drug Abuse

Many teachers and church leaders as well as parents do not want to face the drug problem head on. It frightens them to think that someone might be drunk during an English test or high on grass during the morning sermon. Some school administrators, too, are highly threatened by the drug problem. They, like many ministers, would prefer to gloss over the truth and preserve the image of their institution—and their own image as head of that institution.

Even more subtle are the rumors that we have lost the drug problem, that it has diminished. In actuality, several changes have occurred. Teenagers are using drugs in a more sophisticated manner. Rather than staggering around school, they get loaded at home or at parties; therefore, they don't get caught as often. Barbiturates and amphetamines do not seem to be as frequently used, while heroin, cocaine and particularly alcohol and marijuana are on the increase. Some young people achieve levels of drug usage just below addiction level and can even maintain a light usage of a drug like heroin. While the late sixties may have seemed like a peak in drug abuse, actually the problem in an altered way is still very much with us.

Those of us who are realistic are aware that in spite of the fact that much of the drug problem is well covered up, the only attitude that will help is to assume the problem has not passed us by and to openly work out ways to help young people on drugs.

Nevertheless, many concerned parents, teachers and leaders still ask why. Why would a 14-year-old girl need to live a dual life of smoking grass and getting loaded on alcohol with her friends at parties while going to church every Sunday with her parents who regard her as an ideal, innocent child?

Why would a popular athlete risk his status on the team by secretly dropping pills on the way home from school and smoking grass on weekends?

Why would a student body leader with popularity and academic success use drugs for added kicks and excitement?

Just as there is no typical teenage user or pusher, so also there is no typical, simple reason for drug abuse. The reasons are as varied as the individuals involved. Some use drugs to hurt their parents. Some want to defy authority. Others want a few kicks or need to feel "in" with a particular crowd.

Peter, a conscientious, hard-working college student, began dropping bennies, a kind of "upper," in high school in order to stay awake and study. His goals were unrealistically high and he seemed to have to constantly prove himself. He communicated well with his parents on most subjects, but they did not know he dropped pills to get his grades and hold his jobs. I would not have known either if he had not reached out for help. At school he got along well, both academically and socially. He was not the "type" most people would have suspected of drug abuse, nor was his successful family the "type" to produce the kind of problems which lead to drugs.

Another boy, Marc, was struggling with grades and

34

having a difficult adjustment with his new school. Then, just when things were going better, his girl friend became pregnant by him and he felt a strong obligation to marry her. They subsequently lost the baby and things became strained within the marriage. Marc started smoking pot. After that he did not seem to care about anything anymore. Soon he was divorced and drifting, devoid of any goals or a sense of responsibility to anyone—even himself.

At times the reasons for drug abuse make little sense. A boy who dropped acid regularly began to have bad trips. These frightened him, which, of course, only made the next trips worse. He told me that he knew that some day he might freak out and end up as a permanent inmate of a mental hospital. But still he had to continue to drop acid until he could once again prove he could handle it.

Equally illogical is the student who said: "I don't know much about acid except my sister took it because she thought she was going crazy and she wanted to speed up the process so she'd know, one way or the other. On her third trip she freaked out and spent a week in a mental ward trying to come down off it. That scared . . . me and so I haven't tried it yet, but I think I'm going to 'cause I know I'm going crazy but I won't get the help I need until I'm totally berserk. . . ."

His words "—I won't get the help I need until I'm totally berserk—" still ring in my ears.

Even a legitimate use of drugs can lead to trouble. A girl who stays constantly stoned, first learned what drugs could do when she was sick in the hospital. She says, "Ever since then I have felt that to escape from my problems is to drop a little red pill."

Whatever the reasons, drug and alcohol abuse are symptomatic of deep needs. A former drug user explained, "The world of drugs is a lonely but happy world and drug users rarely admit its wrongs. They are always looking at its good side or just through their point of view. There are so many people taking drugs or hooked on drugs who really don't know why. Some because they're curious, lonely, uncomfortable, want to escape from reality and be somewhere up high where few people reach. Some in search for something they don't know. . . ."

One boy wrote directly about the relationship between the problem of drugs and the void of purposelessness and boredom in life: "I don't always like the idea that I'm a doper, but there is just nothing to do in my free time. I have put down, but there is nothing to do to replace it so I always go back to drugs."

In commenting about modern man's dilemma regarding his purpose in life, Joseph Fabry says: "He [modern man] comes to feel that he is hopelessly gripped by circumstances beyond his control, that he is 'stuck,' that he has been defeated by life, that life is a rat race, a treadmill, and that there is a vast emptiness in him—Frankl's 'existential vacuum.' This vacuum exists among the rich and the poor, the young and the old, the successes and the failures. As logotherapists could show, business executives try to fill it with extra work, their wives with parties and bridge games, students with marijuana or LSD. The existential vacuum lurks behind many of man's feverish attempts to fill his emptiness—with sex, alcohol, defiance of authority, speedy cars, committee work, television watching, overeating, and even with such respected activities as politics, psychoanalysis, and religion. The feeling of emptiness is especially widespread among the youth. Forty percent of Frankl's Austrian students and 81 percent of his American students confessed to it. . . ."[1]

Such feelings do not necessarily force a person to try drugs, but they are one reason young people turn on. At least they feel alive, aware. At least they have experienced *something*.

Self-Esteem: The Basic Problem

More basic to the problems of many teenagers is a lack of self-esteem—a lack which a chemical can temporarily alleviate. I have never yet talked to a drug user who was really comfortable with himself or respected and truly esteemed himself. Some are intelligent, talented and good-looking. But all that seems to make no difference. They do not identify with that "self" they feel is external or projected for other people's benefit. They say, "Yes, but you don't know what I'm *really* like." Or "I have to act good (or be a good student or be a track star or make myself pretty) because no one would like me if I didn't."

Others who do not excel and thus are not recognized, who feel lost in the crowd, cannot perceive that they are worth anything to anyone. "Teachers and parents at least like smart kids. They wish the rest of us weren't around."

Repeatedly, I have heard young people on drugs verbalize their feelings of low self-esteem. "No one will notice me unless I take LSD." "It doesn't matter if I overdose and die. No one likes me anyway." "My family's ashamed of me. I'm so fat and ugly." "I can't seem to do anything right anyway so why shouldn't I get stoned?"

And, more often than not, the teenagers who tell me how ugly, stupid, clumsy, ill-mannered, conceited, bothersome and unlovely they are have many positive qualities they cannot perceive.

Self-esteem is the value one places in himself, the

estimate of his worth. This evaluation is based on two things: first, what the facts are, that is, what there is in a person to evaluate, what he is actually like, how he conducts his life; and second, how the facts are interpreted, that is, how a person perceives or feels what he evaluates.

A person with low self-esteem feels uncomfortable and at odds with himself. He is haunted by his bad habits, faults and weaknesses, yet he may be unable to improve himself because he cannot gain the perspective necessary for change. Self-conscious, he is almost obsessed with what people will think about his actions. He feels inferior to many people, yet because of his inability to cope with these feelings he may act haughty, disdainful and superior to cover them up.

He is unable to accept a compliment and will probably deny it or put himself down in return so that the person who praised him will not be "deluded." Yet he will be crushed if someone puts him down unfairly since he has no realistic self-opinion with which to counteract the false accusation. He feels an urgent need to justify himself and his actions before the world.

He is unsatisfied with who he thinks he is and may spend a lot of time wishing or daydreaming about what it would be like to be someone else or somewhere else. He resents what has been given to him in life and cannot seem to escape his own undesirability.

A young college girl I know is a good example of a person with worth who is unable to perceive that worth. After a childhood of being told she was stupid and the most difficult child of the family, she naturally had a dim view of herself. When I first saw her she told me that she knew she could not go to college and make the grades. Nor did she think she could hold down a job or manage a marriage. In addition, she expressed many negative feelings about how ugly she felt and how rejectable and unlovable she was.

She has now started a part-time job and is taking four classes in college where she is maintaining a B average—to her complete surprise. A teaching career at this point seems a possibility. She told me recently that for the first time in her life she feels worthwhile. It is true that she is now living in a more responsible way and so greater feelings of worth are warranted. Yet even before, she had many positive qualities such as her intellectual capacity, her attractive physical appearance and her pleasant personality which she was unable to accept.

Somehow the facts about her as a person had become distorted. Her parents, early teachers and peers, either unintentionally or cruelly, had probably capitalized on her mistakes—"Don't touch that!"; "Scaredy cat!"; "Why can't you ever be good?"; "Cry baby!"; "No, No, No, No"—all of which she had interpreted as "I can never do anything right"—an attitude which she carried over with her into adulthood.

I have more directly seen this kind of negative conditioning going on in a 15-year-old boy who lives alone with his father. Repeatedly, the father tells me: "Please change Dave. He is terrible to live with—dirty, sarcastic, complaining, unappreciative." Yet the father ignores the value of Dave's superior intellectual capacity and the genuine efforts Dave has made to do some things differently in order to please him. His father only sees the negative, and so Dave only sees the negative, too. He hears his father complain about him and run him down and figures that if his own father cannot stand him, why should he respect himself.

Children brought up with respect will usually learn self-respect and respect for others. Such respect from parents obviously does not mean automatic approval of

39

everything, for that, too, is destructive. But it does mean genuine acceptance of the child's worth potentially and a recognition of his strong points rather than constant reminders of his weaknesses and bad habits.

The most poignant declaration of low self-esteem that I have yet read was written by a boy who outwardly looks forward to a successful life. Talented, studious and envied by many, Bill wrote the following:

"At present my existence has very little meaning or purpose. I get up, I go to school, I come home, I do my homework, I go to bed. At best, I go through the day without getting depressed once. At worst, I feel utterly worthless, totally alone. Unless I am occupied, I start thinking about all the stupid things I have done that day. People try to tell me about all the things I have to live for: money, success, happiness. But how can I have happiness without feeling worthwhile? People think that happiness is being a little smarter than anyone else. Being smarter only makes it harder to make friends. Being smarter only makes it harder to live with yourself and all your ineptness. Nobody likes someone who is smarter than himself. . . . Maybe I should say that my goal in life is to be the greatest musician in the world. But it really isn't. I suppose my goal is to feel worthwhile. Some people would read this and laugh. They are unfeeling and thoughtless. I feel right now like people don't like me, they like my talent. . . . But I want people to like *me*, the person. I want to feel needed."

Many teenagers cannot express their needs as clearly as Bill did. Instead, they code them or act them out. One girl who had talked to me only a few times said one day, "I won't come in and bother you any more. I feel sort of funny when I ask you to help me when you have other kids with much bigger problems." Later, this same girl faked an abortion in order to warrant my attention.

What she and other young people are asking in many ways is "Please care. Please love me."

If we do not care about the teenagers around us, they will reach out to someone else or something else—like drugs. One young person said to me, "Teenagers need to be able to grasp something that says, 'I care.' For many, the dope pushers become this something because the pushers say they care. They care that we're feeling bad. They'll give us something that 'will make us feel great.' " A junior high girl who dropped acid repeatedly said she stopped feeling ugly and envious of others. She became sure of herself as a "completely capable and beautiful creature." Another told me she enjoyed herself only when she was on acid.

Going Up and Coming Down

Sometimes drugs and alcohol are a temporary escape from facing the questions people have about life. At other times young people may actually try to find answers or acceptance through drugs. The results, however, usually prove as unreal as the drug-oriented trip itself. When drug users come down or crash, there are only questions once more, not answers.

One day a boy named Tom walked into the middle of my class and asked me for help. He had dropped acid for the first time and was hysterical. I remember the incident clearly because it was my first experience with a bad LSD trip. I, too, was near panic over what to do, but I managed to conceal that emotion. I knew that any additional stress could set off a panic reaction in him. It is vital that people who become involved with a person on LSD remain accepting and reassuring. It is not the time to warn that person about the dangers of drugs or threaten him in any way. It is certainly not a time to leave him alone. According to Dr. Thomas Ungerleider of UCLA, at the acute stage of LSD intoxication, the person on LSD needs a reassuring "guide" or "sitter." The sitter's job is to convince "the patient that he has not permanently harmed himself and that the effects will wear off. He should never be told he has 'irreparably damaged his brain' (as one LSD user was told when he called an emergency facility for crisis intervention). This promptly precipitated a panic."[2] Many times the difference between this type of experience and a less traumatic one can depend on the understanding and wisdom of those around the person.

Ironically, Tom took the LSD because of peer pressure to prove he was not afraid to try it. Then, when he panicked and turned himself in, his "friends" beat him up.

When his friends talked with me about their cruel treatment of Tom, they felt no remorse, no compassion. They were cold and unrelenting in their feeling that if he could not take it, he did not deserve their friendship. Above all, they assumed he had turned other kids in to the authorities. That, in their world, is unforgivable. In his search for acceptance, Tom had gained just the opposite—rejection.

Not only do young people fail to find permanently valid results from their drug experiences, but many times they are totally unaware of what they are like when they are stoned.

One girl I know who frequently becomes intoxicated usually forgets what has happened after she comes down. When loaded, she tells me how unhappy she is, how miserable alcohol makes her feel. Then when she is normal again, she tells me that she loves the feeling of being drunk and that it makes her happy. She cannot remember how miserable she was or the things she said. She just knows that for a brief span of time she can blot out her awareness of life with alcohol. This is one of the more frustrating aspects of working with drug or alcohol users—trying to convince them of things they cannot remember and do not want to face.

One girl said, "I drink quite often. I tend to feel like a helpless child, not knowing right from wrong while under the influence. My head along with the rest of me seems to get very heavy, and the things going on around me don't seem important at all. In fact, I could care less. My mind seems to go blank at times and I don't remember where I've been or what I've done. I forget things very easy. My speech is all messed up, and the words that I would like to say don't always come out. I can get very mad if I'm bothered. The real bummer is when you come down 'cause you feel worse off than when you started out."

One boy expressed his bitter disappointment with drugs in verse:

Once I lived in the right world to live
And then I went and believed
   what I shouldn't of believed.
Not because I was unhappy,
   not because I was sad.
I only did because they had.

Now I am living in my world all alone
And sure wish I could go back
   to where I once belonged
My friends don't want me, and I see why
But, why must everybody say good-bye?

But I am going away to another world
Maybe it's heaven, maybe it's hell.
I only want to leave this world!

There are experiences which are not nice
This was one of those ones.
It was stupid, stupid indeed.
It was a stupid, stupid "trip."

Another girl states her problem more objectively. "I'm there now. I became really hung up on acid, mescaline and all of the hallucinogenic drugs. Although they helped some, they hurt me too. As the formerly popular Beatles said, 'Acid can open a few doors, but it's not the real answer.' That's what I believe now."

Dreams, Nightmares and Flashbacks
In addition to only perpetuating a teenager's search for worth and purpose, drugs can also produce some rather terrifying experiences along with the good feelings of well-being and security.

One girl described her experience on LSD trips: "On an acid trip I feel very sure of myself, but I feel that the whole world is against me. I feel like a helpless rat at times, trying to hide myself in a corner for fear that people are talking about me. But also there are a lot of beautiful things to remember on an acid trip. For example, music playing. I always remember a song, or a flower, or a sound going on and then repeating it the next day when you're down. . . ."

Severe feelings of claustrophobia were experienced by one boy on LSD. As he entered his bedroom, he felt the walls closing in. He was sure he would be smashed. He tightly closed his eyes, fully believing that the walls would crush him if he opened his eyes. Then, slowly, he stepped backward into the rest of the house where he felt safer.

One young girl who smokes marijuana said that when she is not with her boy friend, she gets "very paranoid and if I can't see things I won't believe they exist. Once I had to have a friend hand me my foot just so I could hold it and know it was there. My mind wanders and after holding my foot I decided that my whole body was severed at the waist and I'd have to waddle around on my hip bones."

Also, with LSD, flashbacks can occur at any time after the original trip. A 17-year-old boy drops acid on a fairly regular basis. One day he came to me for help because he was having a bad flashback. I felt trapped between legal obligations, my teaching schedule and the boy's needs. I could only ask for help from teachers I could trust. After all, who would believe it was just a flashback unless they knew the boy well.

We managed to stay with him and keep him quiet. At one point in the afternoon, Jon decided that writing out his thoughts and feelings would help calm him down:

"I am flashing on acid. The room is doing funny things and my mind's moving slow. Things that are ordinary seem new and different. My body feels like when you run a long way and stop suddenly. There is a feeling in my legs like just after you stretch and yawn. I feel remote somehow, but I know I'm here and I know what I'm doing. I feel ashamed and sorry.... I feel secure because I'm with friends who would not betray me. I'm really messed up.... I have trouble writing and reading and my eyes feel two sizes too large. If two people talk at once it messes me up. Badly...."

A Very Mixed Bag

Other problems also enter the picture. For one thing, drugs that young people buy from each other or even adult pushers are not pure. Capsules can be filled with something harmless like powdered sugar or mixed with some dangerous substance.

One boy had this experience: "It was a Tuesday when I decided to drop some downers. Four for a dollar would cover me all day. After taking them I was feeling tired, mad like to get in a fight and kill. But after a while it paid off because I decided to take one more. But what I didn't realize was I just took an overdose with one-fourth heroin in each one. I was foaming at the jaws. I couldn't walk. I was dizzy and tired. People from the apartments came over and helped me. They threw me in the shower and gave me coffee."

Acid is almost never pure and dosages are never accurate because it is always home-produced. From one trip to the next, its effects are unpredictable.

One week someone sold some high school students joints which contained catnip rather than marijauna. Yet some students thought they were getting high when they smoked them. This situation would be comical except that such lack of uniformity in what teenagers buy and smoke leads to misconceptions which could prove fatal. I know young people who smoke a number of joints with no great effect just because the marijuana is weak. Yet they boast to me about how well they handle marijuana. I have stopped generalizing from what I hear from any individual about the effects of a given amount of marijuana. His experience is only a commentary on his particular supply and his personal chemical and psychological reactions to it.

If a teenager is "burned" and gets powdered sugar in his capsules, he may be in more danger than a teen who gets the pure stuff. The deluded teen may drop a few and feel he can handle them. The next time he may try more and die.

Too, teenagers frequently mix pills with other pills and with alcohol. The results may be extremely dangerous since one pill can set off a catalytic reaction with another or the results can be intensified in the presence of alcohol. No one can accurately predict the seriousness or even the symptoms. I always feel that a person who mixes chemicals in this way is showing me the depths his suffering self-esteem has reached.

It would be difficult to paint too dark a picture about teenage abuse of any drug. Even those who do not overdose or have any bad trips and who stay relatively clear of the entanglements of the drug subculture are into a pattern of living which prevents them from coping with life in a direct way.

Drugs begin a way of life which concentrates on escaping from problems rather than coping with them. The same can be said of the abuse of alcohol and FDA-approved, doctor-prescribed pills. Even with marijuana, legalized or not, to be high is to escape reality. And with marijuana we are a long way from the kind of precise predictions which can be made about dosage and long-term usage of alcohol and pills.

From a long-term point of view, those who have used acid for any amount of time seem to feel that it has an adverse effect on them. They try to verbalize a sensation where they feel that their brain is not functioning the way it used to. Girls worry about chromosome damage. Although teenagers fear drugs, that fear is not an adequate deterrent for most. They hate themselves at times and therefore the thought of death or self-destruction does not usually make them stop taking drugs.

What Can the Helping Adult Do?

Parents who are neither blind to the possibility of *their* child's potential for drug abuse nor overly paranoid about their fears that he might be taking drugs are in a good position to help their own teenagers as well as others. Usually it is hard to know when a teenager is on

47

drugs and what drug he is using. Radical changes in life-style, like excessive sleeping or sleeplessness, abrupt changes in friendships, sudden belligerence, extremes in moodiness *may* indicate a drug problem or indeed some other emotional problem. Such signals are red flag warnings that something may be wrong.

It is important for a parent or teacher to be aware of the symptoms and to wait for the right time to talk, but *never* accuse unless there is absolute proof. The teenager needs to realize that the adult world is not so stupid that it cannot observe the abnormality of his spacing out staring at a light bulb (a good indication of LSD). Yet the average young person reacts violently to abrupt accusations. A better approach is to start with a general inquiry about how the young person feels and with the promise that you are available to talk when and if he is willing.

Tackling the Real Problem

I personally believe that we have reached the point in our drug programs where the scare and even the educational approach are having negligible results. Real success in fighting drug abuse will come only when we as individuals and as a society understand why teenagers use drugs and alcohol and begin to meet some of their basic needs—the needs for worth and purpose in life.

Beth has put down alcohol for several months now. Basically I think she put down because she knew that she was in so deep that if she drank much more, she would have permanent damage. With sheer guts and some help from friends, she made it. But she has still not solved her problems. She feels of little value to other people and perhaps of less value still to herself. In short, she does not accept herself, nor does she feel that life holds any real purpose for her. Why is she here? She does not know. People helped her get off alcohol, but no one successfully gave her anything in its place. So now she says, "Alcohol covered up all the hurt and now it's all out there where I can feel it. Maybe drinking wasn't so bad after all."

The only real way to combat the drug problem is to get at the problems that cause the hurt. The drug abuser does not feel worthwhile nor does he see value and purpose in his life. Therefore, he takes drugs or drinks alcohol—which mask the pain, but increase his feelings of low self-esteem, and hinder him from finding real purpose in life.

Nicki was a girl who had every reason to feel a deep sense of inadequacy. She lived in a home where she was repeatedly rejected by one stepfather after another. Her mother left when she felt like it and returned when it pleased her. In the meantime Nicki became mother to four younger brothers and sisters. Sometimes she would talk to me, put down drugs and then drift away. A few months later, she came back, on drugs again and wanting help.

Then she did something which seemed all wrong, but turned out right. She ran away with her boy friend to a state where they could get married. She was lucky. Tom really loved her and took care of her. Soon she was back in school and went on to get her diploma. Now, two years later, she is still off drugs. She has something positive in their place: a sense of worth and purpose from the love of a husband and baby who need her. When she calls me now, she cannot understand what she saw in drugs or what some of her friends see in them now. She has made it because her real problems have been at least partially solved.

Many students find solutions for their drug problems in their relationship with Jesus Christ. According to one extremely bright 15-year-old, "God is most important because He gives me a purpose for which to live. When I have problems, I don't have to turn to weed or alcohol and destruction of myself and others. This applies to the times when I feel no one loves me or when I am having a hard time in school or home, or when death or disaster hit, or when I am just generally downhearted. I am able to turn to Jesus."

Recently, I heard a former drug addict tell a group of teenagers that his prayer of commitment to Christ was, "Jesus, if you're real (and by real I mean just as real as everything else I've been going through—all the jails and everything else) and if you can change me and if you make me dig living a new kind of life so I don't need to get loaded, so I don't want to because I'm happy without it, then you can have me." The result of that prayer has been over a year of freedom from drugs because Christ Himself has become real.

Marijuana for the teenager, excesses of alcohol for the business executive, abuse of tranquilizers for the housewife or opium for the ancient Chinese philosopher —these are all forms of a universal "solution" to universal problems. When life gets too rough, man either changes that life or succumbs to it and blots out its pain with a chemical. This fact has been true since the beginning of the history of mankind. Cocaine, opium, hashish, alcohol—these are old solutions, not new, as are the basic problems of man's search for himself and his reason for being.

The essential message of Christianity reaches out to drug-abused lives and seeks to communicate that each person has worth—worth enough for the great cost of Christ's coming to earth to redeem him. Worth enough for God to take infinite concern about every detail of human life. Worth enough for God to say that for each of His own, He has plans for a "future and a hope."[3] God challenges us to relate this message of love and hope to our drug-torn culture.

In Summary

1. The drug problem of the late sixties and early seventies has changed but not vanished from a former emphasis on hard drugs to the more socially acceptable pills, LSD, alcohol and marijuana.

2. A sense of emptiness and a low self-image are two major contributing factors in the continuing patterns of teenage drug abuse.

3. Teenagers can conquer drug abuse only by the quality of relationships that can come in a good friendship with a responsible adult and in a deep commitment to Jesus Christ. In essence, Jesus Christ and caring Christians must take the place of the drug pusher and the chemical high.

chapter three
Seeking Help through Psychotherapy

The first time I saw Joe, he was speaking at a high school assembly program. He was black, in his early twenties and a little nervous, but a genuine sincerity rang in his voice as he said simply, "There are two words you are going to hear: Jesus Christ and the Bible."

He went on to tell of himself. Though brought up in a respectable, non-ghetto home, he began to use drugs in his early teens. From grass and pills he went to heroin. And that was where he had been three years earlier when he met Jesus Christ.

He had gone to a friend's house to ask for money for a fix. The friend said that first he must read David Wilkerson's book *The Cross and the Switchblade.* He did and forgot about the money. Later, as a result of that book, he committed his life to Christ. His life was divinely transformed, and he completely conquered his drug addiction.

Now, three years later, our paths crossed, and I found

he was working with some of the same problems as I did with students I knew and cared about. But he knew how to reach them, and I was inexperienced and unsure of myself.

After the assembly, we met and agreed to pool our efforts to a certain degree. For a number of months we did just that. On scheduled days we talked to different groups of students—about anything that interested them: sex, war, grades, death and of course drugs. I could always call on him when I got into a tight spot. Young people who could not trust anyone connected with the academic establishment could trust him. He knew how to handle the hard core user and was especially adept with the pusher. Above all, he supported and reassured me when I needed reassurance in order to continue reaching out to students.

Then, two years after our first meeting, Joe was dead. An overdose of barbiturates was blamed.

Perhaps part of the explanation for Joe's death can be found in looking at those two years. Joe worked relentlessly. He had a gift for working with people; he liked them and understood them. He had no college degree, but he could captivate teenagers in group discussion. "Dopers" knew he was real. And so, when they needed help, they turned to him at any hour of the day or night.

Increasingly, Joe had no life of his own. He kept at it as though there was an endless job to be done and no one else to do it. His relationship with Christ was less apparent and less emphasized. He did not get enough rest. We talked about it, but he could not seem to stop. He could not accept even the physical limitations of being a human being. Feelings of inadequacy began to show through more and more, compensated for by almost compulsive activity. He was not satisfied to help some— he had to help everyone. He became concerned about

54

preserving his image in the community, and to do so required phenomenal energy and time. Certainly these feelings were understandable. After all, it was thrilling as well as frightening to make the transition from a heroin addict, rejected by the establishment, to a leader who commanded great respect from that same establishment.

Then, he died. Some in the drug world said he was phony and they used his death to reinforce their own distorted views. But he was not phony. He was a man, a good man, with spiritual and psychological problems.

From a spiritual point of view he might never have died had he kept up his daily devotional life with Christ. But his low self-esteem made him work so hard that he was too physically tired and emotionally drained to feed his spiritual life.

Man: Body, Mind and Spirit

A human being is a wonderful combination of body and mind and spirit. But no one aspect of him can be ignored or neglected without the others suffering.

A long time ago, C. H. Spurgeon was progressive enough to point out that fatigue can cause spiritual and mental depression. In a sermon Spurgeon preached in England in the late 1800s, he spoke directly regarding the relationship between the body and the mind:

"Certain bodily maladies are fruitful fountains of despondency. And let a man strive as he may against their influence, there will be hours and circumstances in which they will overcome him. . . . These infirmities may be no detriment to a man's career of usefulness. They may even have been imposed upon him by divine wisdom as a necessary qualification for his peculiar course of service. . . . But where in body and mind there are predisposing causes to lowness of spirit, it is no marvel if in dark moments the heart succumbs to them. The wonder in many cases is—and if inner lives could be written, men would see it so—how some keep at their work at all and still wear a smile upon their countenance. Grace has its triumphs and patience its martyrs, martyrs none the less to be honored because the flames kindle about their spirits rather than their bodies, and their burning is unseen by human eyes."[1]

Dr. Martyn Lloyd-Jones comments similarly: "Does someone hold the view that as long as you are a Christian it does not matter what the condition of your body is? Well, you will soon be disillusioned if you believe that. . . . In other words, there are certain physical ailments which tend to promote depression. Thomas Carlyle, I suppose, is an outstanding illustration of this. Or take that great preacher who preached in London for nearly forty years in the last century—Charles Haddon Spurgeon—one of the truly great preachers of all time. That great man was subject to spiritual depression, and the main explanation in his case was undoubtedly the fact that he suffered from a gouty condition which finally killed him. . . . And there are many, I find, who come to talk to me about these matters, in whose case it seems quite clear to me that the cause of the trouble is mainly physical. Into this group, speaking generally, you can put tiredness, overstrain, illness, any form of illness. You cannot isolate the spiritual from the physical for we are body, mind and spirit."[2]

Just as the biochemical, physical part of man can cause emotional problems, so emotional stress and his way of handling that stress can cause physical problems. And, to further complicate things, emotional stress may produce different symptoms, both emotional and physical, in different people. For example, similar traumatic childhood experiences may cause one person to develop a serious personality disorder and give another person ulcers or migraine headaches.

Each of us experiences some physical manifestations of stress. When we get up to make a speech or go to class for an exam, our hands may perspire or our heart beat faster. In times of fear our muscles tighten, our stomach cramps. In addition, for any number of people, stress produces actual ailments, such as peptic ulcers or various skin disorders. But these people rarely consider treatment beyond pain killers or sedatives.

Fear of the Psychological

A bottle of pills seems to make an illness socially and spiritually acceptable, while anything bordering on the psychological is unacceptable and feared. For some reason it is easier for us to accept the effect of the body on the mind or spirit than to accept the effect of the mind on the body and spirit.

One friend of mine who is in her twenties has had an ulcer for years. Finally, about two years ago, her condition became so severe that she had to have a part of her stomach removed. At that point, I all but begged her to seek some professional counseling, but she refused. Yet as I watch her in her compulsively active life, grabbing coffee and hastily prepared meals while she runs from one activity to another, I feel increasingly convinced that at least a part of her stomach symptoms are psychogenic. But she cannot accept the psychological implications of her illness.

Recently a young bookkeeper was suddenly rushed to the hospital with what appeared to be a possible brain tumor. During the few days when tests were being taken, her friends, both Christian and non-Christian, were solicitous and concerned. Everyone spoke of her good points and how sad the situation was.

Then the diagnosis changed. What appeared to be a tumor was the culmination of a long period of somewhat secretly-endured migraine headaches. The concern dropped. Now everyone began to analyze her problems behind her back and pick apart her weaknesses. People stopped asking her how she felt and no one offered sympathy when she obviously felt bad. They acted as though she was responsible for the headaches now that she did not have a tumor, and that she should simply have the will power to stop them. While there was sympathy for her physical ailment, there was only rejection for her psychological problem.

This attitude of disregarding or masking emotional problems and rejecting those who have them (as though most of us did not have them at one time or another) is revealed in many ways—fear, denial, deception, spiritualizing.

The summer after my graduation from college, I met a girl of twenty-two who was interested in becoming a missionary. She had been married and divorced and had lost her baby to her former husband. She had no family and no money, but a well-known missionary had agreed to let her go back with her to Asia as a missionary— "Working in a foreign country will be ideal for her."

As I got to know her, I began to realize the depth of her problems. At that time in my life, I was too young, untrained and prejudiced against the psychological hangups of others to be of much help. But I did try. I took her to a Christian doctor. He was annoyed, cold, administered a sedative and dismissed her as a psychological case. I took her to a Bible study where the Bible teacher told me that all that was wrong with her was "self" and "sin," that she should pray and read the Bible more.

If her problem had been physical, the doctor would

have put himself out to help her, for he is the kind of doctor who still makes house calls even in the middle of the night. If she had been dying of cancer, she would have been helped and loved at the Bible study. But because her problems were psychological, she was shunned and left untreated. And when her problems became too blatantly obvious even to those who did not try to see them, the missionary dropped her without explanation and sought out someone else.

Finally, after preventing her from a suicide attempt, in desperation I deposited her on the doorstep of an elderly retired missionary. There she received some help because this lady was unique in her warmth and caring for people even though she did not always understand them. She loved Christ so much that, although I doubt that she had ever really weighed the balance between psychological and spiritual problems, she was able to reach out in love. However, her help for my friend could only be temporary since she had neither the training nor the time to really effect a change of any depth. And as far as I know, my friend was never given the opportunity for psychotherapy. The last time I saw her, she was an emotionally damaged person.

Granted, it is not easy to distinguish between the spiritual and the psychological. Evidence of spirituality can even sometimes be a mask for emotional problems. A young friend of mine is a literal slave for various ministers and missionaries home on furlough. She cleans for them, washes their clothes and baby-sits their children. People who see and experience her self-giving may well envy her spirituality.

But my friend has problems. She does not like herself well enough to get nice clothes or fix her hair or enjoy herself on an occasional night out. She turns to me and says, "No one loves me." It would seem that at least some of her motivation for helping others is based on deep feelings of inadequacy. She tries to buy love by being everyone's slave. Her spiritual condition before God may be fine, but she still needs to be helped to see that she herself is worthwhile and that she does not have to prove it. To develop such feelings of worth usually requires professional help. Once my friend has a basic amount of self-esteem, her motivation for helping others will begin to arise more out of love for God and out of the normal satisfaction that any human being gets from helping someone.

If Joe, the former addict, could have received psychological care, he might have developed a higher sense of self-esteem and he might have been able to slow down. He would not have felt such a compulsive need to prove himself to the world and, above all, to himself.

The Importance of Self-Esteem

Self-acceptance and self-esteem are not anti-Christian. There is no virtue in thinking you are ugly when you are not. Or a raging beauty when you are average in looks. There is no virtue in thinking you are stupid when you are intelligent. Or a genius when you have a normal I.Q. Since God is a God of truth, we can be sure that he wants us to honestly evaluate ourselves.

Kenneth Wuest translates Romans 12:3 in a way which emphasizes the idea of honest evaluation: "For I am saying through the grace which is given to everyone who is among you, not to be thinking more highly of one's self, beyond that which one ought necessarily to be thinking, but to be thinking with a view to a sensible appraisal (of one's self) according as to each one God divided a measure of faith."[3]

It is true that before God each human being must acknowledge himself as sinful. The Bible teaches that "all have sinned and fall short of the glory of God."[4] Finite man looks pretty ridiculous comparing himself with an infinite God. Yet there is a difference between viewing our worthless moral condition before God and evaluating our worth and potential as human beings.

Humility before God certainly does not make it necessary to propagate or even tolerate self-hate. Christ told his followers to "love your neighbor as yourself."[5] The obvious implication is that they had some basic respect for themselves.

Dr. Rollo May in his book *Man's Search for Himself* has said, "In the circles where self-contempt is preached, it is of course never explained why a person should be so ill-mannered and inconsiderate as to force his company on other people if he finds it so dreary and deadening himself. And furthermore the multitude of contradictions are never adequately explained in a doctrine which advises that we should hate the one self, 'I,' and love all others, with the obvious expectation that they will love us, hateful creatures that we are; or that the more we hate ourselves, the more we love God who made the mistake, in an off moment, of creating this contemptible creature, 'I.' "[6]

A friend of mine who spent about a year in psychotherapy surprised me the other day. He said he felt secure with his therapist only when he was paying for the time. If the therapist gave him any extra minutes when that hour was over, he became nervous. He did not feel worth the gift of extra time. Certainly this is not the view God wants us to have of ourselves. Nor does it foster spiritual growth.

Actually the idea that Christians should dislike themselves is in direct contradiction to the Bible. God places great worth upon man—so much that he was willing to die for him. The sacrifice of Christ and the resultant gift of eternal life made possible by his resurrection are staggering. Certainly God places more worth on us than we can even imagine.

One girl I know, who has taken large amounts of every drug except heroin, shows her self-hate openly. She burns herself with cigarette butts. She is always saying something like, "I'm stupid and ugly and even my family can't stand me." Then, when anyone compliments her or points out some of her strengths, she becomes angry and cuts them off. During the period of time I have known her, she has insulted me, shocked me with stories of her behavior and wanted me to see her stoned on every drug imaginable—to "prove" to me that she is worthless. She tries to make me agree with her low opinion of herself. She has told me repeatedly that I am the only human being who has not agreed with her and sooner or later she will convince me of her worthlessness and hopelessness.

This girl needs Christ and the direction that only a relationship with Him involves. But she also needs psychological treatment to help erase all the unrealistic layers of self-hate which exist in her.

What is so true of drug users and teenage alcoholics is also true of many teenagers who do not turn on. Because of many factors in our society we are producing a generation of young people who are filled with doubts about themselves and life in general. Outwardly they sometimes look so sure, so positive that they are right. Inwardly they are often scared to death, confused and hopeless.

Ministering to the Total Man

Parents and those of us who work with young people, particularly those on drugs, must be careful to ask for wisdom in determining how to treat problems. It takes divine balance to know when a problem is spiritual or physical or psychological. It is even harder to know when it is a combination. To really help, we must give answers that suit the problem—spiritual for spiritual, physical for physical, psychological for psychological. The help given in each area need not conflict. We are working for the unity, the well-functioning, of the whole man.

Although there is a gradual shifting of attitudes within even the most conservative circles, many people continue to have a fearful distrust of mental illness and of help for mind-related problems. This attitude defies logic. For the person with physical problems, we combine prayer with good medical care. For the person with emotional problems, we tend to reject good psychological care, treating completely with spiritual "answers." We exhort people to "trust God more" or to "deal with the sin in their lives" and then, if the symptoms do not obligingly disappear, we conclude that their spiritual life is inadequate. (And if we have any conscience at all, we feel a sense of guilt because we couldn't help them.)

Why Parents Refuse Help

Parents, especially, have a hard time facing it when their children develop emotional problems. They rationalize and do almost anything to keep from admitting what they feel reflects their own failure.

John is the son of a minister in a moderately active local church. He is a good, hard-working student. His peers admire his abilities and envy him because they think that having a minister for a father means John has someone to talk to. But John can't talk to his father.

When his feelings of anger and anxiety became unbearable one day, John came into my office. His exterior was calm, almost cheerful. Yet he kept pleading with me to believe that it was all a front, that inside he was confused and unhappy. He said he could not stand it any more.

Getting his feelings out helped some. But then the emotion built again, and again. Finally I recommended professional counseling at a local agency. John agreed. I proceeded to make preliminary arrangements with the agency. There was no cost to the family.

When John asked his parents to sign the consent paper, they refused. Why? Because John's mother had once been in a mental hospital. In their minds, for John to go to a counselor meant he would end up in a mental hospital. It meant he had big problems. Their philosophy seemed to be that if you hid a problem long enough, it would go away.

Somewhere, about fifteen years before, John's mother had asked for the same help John was now pleading for. She was turned down. A whole family tried to pretend the problem did not exist. I expected them to have learned from the mother's experience. I thought that this time they would be sympathetic to emotional problems, that they would want to get help sooner. But I was wrong. John is not getting help even though he needs and wants it.

Some parents refuse help for their children because they are afraid of what the child will tell the therapist, that their family life will be portrayed in a bad light. While everyone desires a certain amount of privacy, to keep it at the expense of the mental health of one's own children is to keep it at an exorbitant price.

But perhaps the most common reason parents refuse psychotherapy for their children is that they cannot deal with their own guilt feelings. They feel responsible. They cannot forgive themselves for raising imperfect children. Yet when their children develop physical ailments, such as thyroid conditions, hemophilia or metabolic diseases like diabetes, which many doctors feel have hereditary bases, those same parents accept these physical problems with less trauma.

Every human being is a combination of weaknesses and strengths, partially given to him through his genes and influenced for better or worse through environmental causes. No man can claim to be all strong or all weak. Nor will he see all his strengths or all his weaknesses duplicated in his child. His strength may be his child's weakness, and vice versa. There is often no more reason for guilt if a child develops emotional problems than if in the course of his life physical illnesses occur.

The real guilt that parents should feel, and frequently do not, is the guilt of ignoring or playing down a real problem which could be eliminated or helped if it were faced and worked through early enough. Instead, many parents lay the foundation for future years of guilt: Their children grow up with faulty self-images, have joyless and unfulfilling marriages and produce children who continue to reflect both the grandparents' and parents' hang-ups.

A parent who must rely on superficial roles to relate successfully to other people will not be able to help his child develop confidence in his own ability to be liked as he is. A woman who is insecure about her female image will not encourage her daughter to be accepting of her own femininity. Usually in ways they are completely unaware of, parents who have an unsatisfactory sex life instill negative ideas about sex—that it is dirty or unpleasant or threatening—in the minds of their children. The real guilt of these parents comes when they refuse to let others help their child when they themselves cannot or do not. A parent is responsible to see that his child is as well defended against psychological

65

illness as possible. Furthermore, a parent should see that his child receives help when he needs it.

Psychotherapy and Christians

Perhaps added to the average Christian's uneasiness about counseling is the fear that psychotherapy itself is somehow evil and out to corrupt Christian beliefs. A young boy, the son of a minister, who was in therapy with a Christian psychologist, came into my office one day. Before he sat down or even told me why he had come, he asked me a list of questions: "Are you a Christian, a real born-again Christian? Do you believe in the Trinity? Do you believe in the virgin birth?" He was almost in a state of panic that I would corrupt his Christian faith.

This fear of spiritual corruption is based on a mistaken idea that counselors, and particularly psychologists and psychiatrists, are out to subvert Christians from their beliefs. This is the age-old fear of anything "secular." Such people feel they can trust only Christian doctors, mechanics, writers, grocers, newscasters, therapists. And the caricatures and distortions of the psychiatric profession shown in movies, in which morality is not stressed or is put aside altogether, does not allay their fears.

In actuality, while some therapists are anti-Christian, a great many do not tamper with the religious beliefs of their patients. Objectivity demands that they accept the patient with whatever beliefs he has and then work within that framework. Frequently, good therapy will produce a healthier emotional state in which the development of one's spiritual life can flourish.

Nevertheless, the stigma of psychotherapy exists. Typical of this attitude is the following generalization made by a minister: "Some of you pay $50.00 a week to go to a psychiatrist who tells you you're not as bad or guilty as you think you are." The minister, for whom I normally have high regard, then went on to advise his audience to "take their problems to the Lord" instead. The minister misled his people in two ways. First, he failed to understand what good psychotherapy can do: that it can help a person become able to make better decisions and actually raise the level of his responsibility.

C. S. Lewis says it well: "Imagine three men who go to war. One has the ordinary natural fear of danger that any man has and he subdues it by moral effort and becomes a brave man. Let us suppose that the other two have, as a result of things in their subconsciousness, exaggerated, irrational fears, which no amount of moral effort can do anything about. Now suppose that a psychoanalyst comes along and cures these two: that is, he puts them both back in the position of the first man. Well, it is just then that the psychoanalytical problem is over and the moral problem begins. Because, now that they are cured, these two men might take quite different lines. The first might say, 'Thank goodness I've got rid of all those doo-dahs. Now at last I can do what I always wanted to do—my duty to the cause of freedom.' But the other might say, 'Well, I'm very glad that I now feel moderately cool under fire, but, of course, that doesn't alter the fact that I'm still jolly well determined to look after Number One and let the other chap do the dangerous job whenever I can. Indeed one of the good things about feeling less frightened is that I can now look after myself much more efficiently and can be much cleverer at hiding the fact from the others.' Now this difference is a purely moral one and psychoanalysis cannot do anything about it. However much you improve the man's raw material [the various feelings, impulses and

67

so on which his psychological outfit presents him with], you have still got something else: the real, free choice of the man, on the material presented to him, either to put his own advantage first or to put it last. And this free choice is the only thing that morality is concerned with. The bad psychological material is not a sin but a disease. It does not need to be repented of, but to be cured."[7]

Second, the minister failed to make the important distinction between real and neurotic guilt. Real guilt has a spiritual answer in the forgiveness Christ offers. Real guilt is and should be experienced when we act wrongly, when we lie, gossip, steal and so on. In real guilt the problem is spiritual and the guilt leaves when it is dealt with spiritually. "If we confess our sins, he is faithful and just, and will forgive our sins. . . ."[8] This is God's remedy for sin and its resultant guilt.

But neurotic guilt is different. While it can certainly be helped spiritually, it should also receive psychological treatment. For example, a young teenage girl spent her formative years on the mission field with her parents. During her later school years, she suddenly found herself thrust out from her home, alone in a "foreign" stateside school. She broke down emotionally and had to be committed to a hospital. When she came to my office after her discharge from the hospital, she told me of her anger toward her father and her deep, almost consuming guilt over that anger. She said she confessed the sin of anger continually, but had no peace about it.

I tried to show her from the Bible that anger is not necessarily a sin, that it is what we do with anger that determines whether or not we sin. The Bible teaches, "Be ye angry, and sin not."[9] I pointed out that Christ showed anger to the money changers in the temple and to the Pharisees and Sadducees numerous times. But it was difficult to convince her that she could be honest about her feelings toward her father and not be sinning. She had, at least in part, a neurotic sense of guilt. And her false sense of guilt filled her with feelings of self-loathing, which further damaged her emotional health.

Facing Up to Reality

Having an emotional problem does not necessarily imply sin. So if a person develops problems of a psychological nature, it should cause no more guilt than many other adverse situations which confront people as they go through life. A person does not generally feel guilt over a case of pneumonia or a bad heart. Nor does he blame himself because he cannot always be first in his class or immediately at the top of the business or professional world.

Having an emotional problem is not something to hide or be ashamed of. It merely indicates there are needs not being met—needs which perhaps never have been met.

It is usually people who have the greatest needs who deny they have any problems. Most psychotic people, for example, do not of their own accord walk into a therapist's office. It seems very hard for people to say, "I have an emotional problem and I need help."

In a class of students with psychological and neurological problems, I had a boy who constantly visited, and should have been part of the class—he had problems similar to those of others in the group. He came to me for help, but he always told me how "weird" the other students were and how superior to them he was. I tried to convince him to join us by pointing out his truly strong points which were indicated in the testing he had had. Or I tried to show him the irrationality of his prejudice. It is the weakest people who hide from help for their problems.

I often use the following story to illustrate this premise. Two young men, just starting out in the business world, are offered positions leading to great advancement. Both have a phobia of height and are therefore afraid to fly on airplanes. Since the positions involve a great deal of travel, each has to decide what to do about his fear. The first man decides to seek psychotherapy to overcome his fear so he can accept the job. The other, while loudly proclaiming nothing is wrong with him, decides to turn down the job because he cannot go through with the travel. I ask young people to tell me which man is "crazier." The answer is usually obvious and puts in a weak position the argument that a person has to be crazy to be in therapy.

Actually, many people seek psychological help for a great variety of reasons: academic difficulties, problems with their jobs, marital problems, physical illnesses related to emotional needs, an immediate crisis, such as a death in the family, or even just a desire to know themselves better.

Choosing a Therapist

Now, suppose a person has become aware of his emotional problems and has decided to trust a professional counselor to help him work them out. Where does he go from here?

Choosing a therapist is not easy, but one basic guideline should be kept in mind: More important than whether the therapist is a psychologist or psychiatrist is his philosophy of treatment—psychoanalytic, behavioristic or existential.

Psychoanalysis stresses insight particularly relating to the cause and effect of one's past on present problems. Behaviorism stresses desensitization techniques and attempts to change behavior by the repetition of positive

70

feedback. A psychoanalyst will attempt to change feelings and attitudes in order to change behavior, while a behaviorist will try to change behavior in order to change feelings.

If a patient has a fear of heights, the psychoanalyst would help him explore the reasons for the fear, usually relating them to childhood trauma. The behaviorist would structure a series of episodes in which the patient gradually experiences more and more threatening heights, remaining at each level until he overcomes his fear.

Differing from both psychoanalysis and behaviorism, existential psychology emphasizes the need of finding oneself and one's place in the universe. Existentialist Viktor Frankl asserts: "Everyone has his own specific vocation or mission in life: everyone must carry out a concrete assignment that demands fulfillment. Therein he cannot be replaced, nor can his life be repeated."[10]

Newer forms of therapy emphasize a variety of philosophies and methods. Increasingly among these is an emphasis on responsibility and need fulfillment.

Furthermore, the therapists I know who seem to be effecting actual changes in people get involved to the point of genuinely caring about their patients' welfare. One man I know who had been in and out of therapy and hospitals finally went to a psychologist of the behavioristic school who believes in a caring involvement with his patients. For one month the therapist saw him every day. Then, probably because the man had already spent so much money, the psychologist did not charge for that month's therapy. Later when the patient was out of therapy, the therapist would call or write a card to keep up the relationship. Today the man is still functioning well.

In choosing a therapist, a person should not be reticent to question his philosophy and technique. People who have been in therapy or who are in contact with therapists can answer some of these questions. But, ultimately, it is necessary to have a session with the therapist under consideration and ask him how he views the nature of therapy, people's religious beliefs, probable length of therapy and anything else which seems important to the potential patient.

In a sense one must depend on his own intuition in the choice of a therapist. One young girl who recognized her need for therapy went to three men before settling on the last one. The first, a Christian psychologist, told her that she thought too highly of herself, that she had been used to being "a large frog in a tiny pond." He said she should enlarge her "pond" by getting into a group and exposing her weaknesses. Even though her awareness of her problems at that time was not great, she knew enough to realize that her problem was one of low, not high, self-esteem, and that therapy with this man could be destructive. Her second choice posed as a Christian, but his Christianity seemed dubious and his suggestions unhelpful. The third man was warm and seemed genuinely concerned about what she said and thought, and she began a fruitful period of sessions with him.

Just as there are helpful and destructive people in every profession, there are also various degrees of proficiency among psychotherapists. It is important for a person to trust his own feelings enough to refuse therapy from someone whom he feels he cannot agree with or trust enough to receive help.

It takes time to develop a good therapeutic relationship, and if one feels he has made a wise choice in his therapist, he should invest the time, money and effort to make a meaningful relationship. When a good relationship between a psychologist and his patient does not develop, there should probably be a change of therapists.

Too many people assume automatically that if things do not work out, the therapist must be right and the patient wrong. While this may sometimes be true, sometimes the therapist is at fault.

One young woman stayed for six months with a psychologist whom she found difficult to talk to and who told her to vent her anger by telling off her friends and husband with whom she was already having serious problems. Although she was a bright person, she tolerated the situation until she was forced through external circumstances to change therapists. Then she discovered that all therapists are not alike and not all equally helpful.

One should keep in mind the fact that one good therapist may not be able to reach certain people that another good therapist may help greatly. Their personalities may not mesh, the therapist himself may not feel confident about his success in handling the kind of problem that the patient presents or one person may not respond to a certain approach which another person would thrive on. In the end one must sort out from the various approaches the one which best suits his needs and, of the therapists who use that approach, the one to whom he can best relate.

"I See You in My Eyes"

There is no doubt that the caring of a good therapist in a warm relationship can make an essential difference in a person's life.

A psychologist in the children's ward at a state hospital had been working for a number of months with an autistic[11] six-year-old boy, Mike. At first, Mike could only relate to inanimate objects like airplanes or boats.

73

Then as time passed by, he became aware of some living things, such as butterflies. And part of the therapy sessions involved chasing countless butterflies, and eventually birds, that were never caught.

Yet Mike was still trapped in an imaginary world of his own. Unable to even accept his own identity, he referred to himself as "Mike," never as "I" or "me." He would say, "Mike wants water" or "Mike is tired." Nor could he relate enough to other human beings to even gain direct eye contact. Instead he would look through them or around them, never at them. His growth in connecting with the reality of the world around him was slow.

Then one day after an exhausting chase around the grounds of the institution, Mike and the therapist collapsed together on the grass to rest. As he turned toward the therapist, suddenly Mike's eyes focused directly into the therapist's. With genuine delight, he said, "*I* see you in *my* eyes!"

Both the frailty and strength of a human being are equally awe-inspiring. How vulnerable we all are to criticism and rejection—and how deeply affected by acceptance. The skillful therapist is able to use that human vulnerability by changing its focus from rejection to acceptance and feelings of worth.

In Summary

1. Each person is composed of body, mind and spirit, and unless each of the three are tested, true wholeness is not generally achieved.

2. Emotional problems in teenagers or adults cannot simply be labeled as sin. Indeed, helping toward their solution offers counselors and parents fertile ground for their own development of spiritual depth and compassion. Few people can effectively help others unless they

themselves have first experienced hurt and some measure of healing.

3. Healthy self-esteem is a quality God wants each Christian to value in proper perspective with biblical teaching on humility and pride.

4. Although not all psychotherapy is helpful, when used correctly it can be a God-given tool the Lord frequently uses to help heal, and should be accepted and used as such.

chapter four

The Dynamics of the Counseling Relationship

One day about two years ago a girl who usually seemed happy came to my office and asked if I would set aside some time later in the day to talk with her. When she came back, I noticed her hands were shaking. She told me that for some weeks, in the middle of classes or meals, she would start shaking or crying for no apparent reason. She could not think of anything in her life which should be causing her problem; and as she talked, I could not explain it either.

Granted, her background was complicated—a broken home, an alcoholic parent, and placement in a foster home about three years earlier. All of these conditions were undoubtedly at the root of her present problem, but we could not uncover an immediate cause. Obvious precipitating causes in this girl's case could have been a shift to a new foster home or a break-up of her current foster home. But none of these things had happened. Her home was stable and she was happy there.

For a while I saw her once a week. We talked about college and a career. We discussed her relationships within the foster family, her concern over worrying them with her problems, her happiness that they accepted her as one of the family, her excitement over a wedding or a birthday in the family. Sometimes we just conversed casually about school—how impossible her government class was or how the greatest boy in the world had just asked her out. She always came promptly and seemed to enjoy the talks. And in a few weeks the shaking and crying had vanished, and she was acting like herself again.

Usually when I talk to someone for a period of weeks or months and begin to see improvement, some reasons for that improvement become clear along with a certain amount of insight into the original causes of the problem. But the fact that neither of us knows what immediate factors in her life brought on the symptoms, and yet there was improvement which has lasted for two years now, shows that insight into causes is not essential to helping someone through his problems—although it is, of course, helpful and reassuring.

What we did have for the nine months when we talked regularly, and still have now on an informal basis, was a good relationship—an involvement with each other where she could trust me because she knew I cared about her and had faith in her ability to make a rewarding, fulfilling life for herself. And because I cared about her and believed in her, in some gradual and maybe unconscious way she began to have more faith in herself. After all, her home situation prior to the foster home had been filled with rejection, and all of that now had to be counteracted by people who accepted her and could make her feel she was a worthwhile and likable person.

Mutual Care, Mutual Awareness

Psychiatrist Dr. William Glasser in his book *Reality Therapy* explains that "at the time any person comes for ... help, he is lacking the most critical factor for fulfilling his needs, a person whom he genuinely cares about and who he feels genuinely cares about him."[1] He maintains that the relationship need not be direct, as a parent to a child or a teacher to a pupil, but that the essential ingredient is that "we have a strong feeling of his existence and he, no matter how distant, has an equally strong feeling of our existence."[2]

The kind of relationship which must exist in any good counseling, parent-child or teacher-child relationship is mutual caring and mutual awareness of that caring. The mutual awareness is vital. A girl who talked to me after two suicide attempts told me that I was the only person who believed in her and thought she had any chance of succeeding in life. Yet her mother had expressed feelings of interest and concern which apparently the girl could not really believe. All the caring in the world does not count for much unless the object of that concern can be made to feel and believe it.

Involvement with others and the resultant effect on a person's self-image begins early in life with one's parents. In fact, the kind of involvements children have with their parents in the early years has a profound influence on their development of personal identity. Children who are surrounded by acceptance and love are more likely to grow up feeling acceptable and lovable. Children who hear "John isn't smart like his brother" or "Why can't you ever do anything right?" or "You're just like your rotten father" will tend to feel unacceptable and unlovable. It is this kind of negative reinforcement that many young people receive in their homes from the time they are born. Eventually they must either come to agree with their parents' statements about their stupidity and worthlessness or else reject the parents as significant persons in their life and seek positive reinforcement elsewhere.

The most destructive treatment a child can receive is the opposite of any involvement—indifference. Research sociologist Morris Rosenberg says, "Whether one belongs to the upper, upper-middle, low-middle, or lower social classes; whether one is a Protestant, Catholic, or Jew; whether one is male or female; whether one lives in a large city, a medium sized community, or a small town—whichever of these conditions obtain, the result is essentially the same: if the parents manifest indifference to the child, that child is less likely to have a high level of self-regard."[3]

In an interesting way, a child who is being ignored by a significant person in his life will often intuitively reach out for a substitute relationship. One nine-year-old youngster whom I saw a few weeks after he had been abandoned by his mother showed his hurt by avoiding any reference to her, both verbally and in drawings. Then several weeks later, he came in happy and told me that he liked his new baby-sitter because "she acts like she's my mother." From that time on, the child improved.

If a child's early relationships directly affect his developing self-image, it is also obvious that a teenager's continuing relationships with people either confirm or tend to change that same self-image. And the reinforcement that is so often used in a negative way in the home can be turned and used as an invaluable tool in counseling. If a young person respects me, I then become a significant person in his life and as such I can have a positive influence on his thinking about himself. My gift of time means, first of all, that he is important. Then if I believe he is important, if I trust him, if I recognize his abilities and if I can show him that my view of him is realistic and substantiated by others, he will slowly begin to believe more and more of my positive valuation of his worth. His feelings about himself will change because of my positive reinforcement.

Teri was an unhappy young girl who had moved from one school to the next during most of her life. By the time I knew her, she was sixteen. Most of the time she looked unkempt and pathetic. She was currently living with an older sister who found the often moody teenager more than she could cope with. Teri frequently came in to talk with me when she was in one of her depressed moods.

Unlike some teenagers, Teri was acutely aware of her low self-esteem. We had long discussions in which I tried to prove her worth to her, and she, in turn, told me why she was worthless. Even though I knew I could not talk her out of feeling worthless, I was relying on continual restatement of the truth to eventually erase some of the negative reinforcement she had heard all her life.

Teri's reasons for hating herself were simple, obvious to her and frustratingly difficult to refute. She had grown up with four fathers who had all, in one way or another, rejected her. Some had mistreated her; others had left. Her mother, a legal secretary, was too busy patching up her own life and maintaining her job to do anything much for her children. Naturally she was not worthwhile, Teri reasoned, or someone would have loved her enough to stay with her and care for her. In essence, her relationships, or lack of them, had effectively proved to her that she was not worth caring about.

By the time Teri was in high school, she had begun to write to her real father. He said he was interested in her and tried in small ways to prove it. She was excited, and

I felt a sense of relief for her. She talked about living with her father and asked him for advice. She began assuming he would be there to help pay for senior pictures or accept charges for a collect phone call when she needed him. In short, she stopped testing him to see if he cared and began to accept the idea without needing further proof.

But when it came to actually allowing Teri to live with him, her father told me that his involvement could not go that far. Teri closed up and stopped trusting. Once again someone who said he cared acted differently in the long run. There was no dramatic collapse, just the old pattern of moodiness, depression and verbalized feelings of self-hate. And it became just that much harder for me to make her believe that I would not desert her, too. Her father was still the most significant person in her life, and his rejection of her mattered more than my acceptance.

Christ's Capacity for Involvement

One of the strongest examples to illustrate the need to be involved with people we are trying to help is Christ Himself as He lived as a man on this earth.

Christ's capacity for involvement enabled Him to notice and care about an immoral woman, to heal lepers cast out by refined society and to save a condemned thief who was crucified on the cross next to Him. He was capable of loving these whom respectable, religious people rejected. This capacity to feel and love and care about another human being is the epitome of Christlike living.

At his trial, Charles Manson is quoted as having said: "Most of the people at the ranch that you call the 'family' were just people that you did not want, people that were alongside the road. Their parents kicked them out so I did the best I could and took them on my garbage dump. . . ."[4]

Yet Christ makes us pointedly aware of His feelings about Manson's "garbage dump" of human lives when He says, "I have not come to call the respectable people, but the outcasts."[5]

And the end result of the relationships which Christ formed was usually a positive personality change in the people He knew. Nowhere is this shown more clearly than in the lives of the disciples with whom He was closest. They were, to start with, ordinary men. Peter was a fisherman, impulsive, fearful to the point of denying Christ prior to His crucifixion. Yet in his ministry he was bold, unafraid and eventually crucified for his faith in Christ. James and John were also common people, who during their time with Jesus Christ dared to suggest that they should both have the highest position with Him. Showing a similar insecurity, the other ten disciples were angry and all twelve showed their jealousy. Yet these same men later became brave and dependable. James believed in Christ to the point of death at the hand of King Herod. John became the one who was called "the disciple whom Jesus loved" and was the one to whom Christ delegated the care of His mother when He was on the cross.

It is impossible to overemphasize the place of the spiritual in the changes of these men. The Bible clearly states that their lives were transformed by the power of God through the indwelling Holy Spirit. Yet it is also impossible to think that the formation of a close, trusting relationship with Jesus as He walked on this earth had no effect on the self-esteem of His disciples.

And in somewhat the same way the relationships we form with the young people we attempt to help may be a vehicle through which God can in a supernatural way touch their lives as well as have a positive psychological effect on the way they view themselves.

Alleviating the Loneliness

In connection with the development of a positive self-image, another important result of involvement is the alleviation of the *aloneness* which often accompanies a person with problems.

When I ask students to talk or write about the thing which frightens them most, almost all of them say they are afraid of being alone in this world.

One tenth-grade boy wrote:

> You can see the fire
> And feel the loneliness around you;
> You can hear the sounds
> But don't know what to do.
>
> You take a look around you
> Hoping someone's near;
> But then you know there isn't,
> It's just your hanging fears.
>
> You wonder what is happiness
> That you have never had;
> You know you will never have it
> Because people think you're bad.
>
> You wish there was someone to talk to,
> Someone part of you,
> You think of all the good times you
>   could have
> And all the things you could do.
>
> But you know this is not possible

You know that it's a lie;
So you say to yourself: "... all the people,
... all the world." And go somewhere
Lie down ... and die.

A short time ago a girl who had just begun to drop
acid came in to talk. She had been to a party the previ-
ous weekend where she and her boy friend had taken
LSD. For him it was one trip too many. He had been
institutionalized. Still shaken by the experience, she
handed me a paper, written while she was on her trip,
and asked me to read it later. It started out like this: "I'm
just so restless I don't know what to do. I feel so deserted
and alone, and the want to survive I feel is slowly van-
ishing away.... I have never felt so alone and empty
before. As I sit outside and watch the things going on,
I feel like it is a turmoil to no destination...."

Many teenagers feel alone in a similar way. And there
are certainly spiritual answers to the feeling of aloneness. Jesus once said, "No, I will not abandon you or
leave you as orphans in the storm."[6] On another occasion he said, "... I am with you always, even to the end
of the world."[7] When we communicate this message to
young people, we will be amazed at the comfort and
help it will bring to their lives.

However, God has created us with a need for human
as well as divine companionship. It is God Himself who
said, "It is not good for the man to be alone,"[8] and then
provided a wife for Adam. Repeatedly throughout the
Scriptures the need for friends is shown. Paul frequently
asked for one of his friends to accompany him, particularly at the end of his life when he seemed to lean rather
heavily on Timothy. At the end of 2 Timothy, he said
to Timothy, "Do your best to come before winter."
Earlier in the same letter he commented on Onesipho-

rus, "because he cheered me up many times. He was not ashamed that I am in prison, but as soon as he arrived in Rome he started looking for me until he found me. May the Lord grant him to receive mercy from the Lord on that Day! And you know very well how much he did for me in Ephesus."[9]

Christ Himself asked His closest disciples to accompany Him and wait for Him when He went to the garden of Gethsemane to pray. He was to be temporarily separated from His heavenly Father by the sins of the world which He was about to bear. Consequently, He felt an agonizing aloneness. He said to Peter, James and John, "Remain here and keep watch"; And then, when they failed, "Could you not keep watch for one hour?"[10]

A few nights ago, a fifteen-year-old girl called and woke me from a deep sleep. Apologetically she blurted out, "I'm sorry to call so late, but I want to take some pills so badly."

Months before we had agreed on a plan: She should learn to substitute people for pills. Since then, whenever she feels like taking something, she calls instead and we talk until the feeling passes. She trades the pills for the feeling of worth that she gets from knowing that she is not alone, that someone does care.

Involvement with other people is risky, for you can be hurt when the people you care for do not care back. The risk is especially great if you are a parent trying to help a child you love. Involvement is time-consuming for the counselor. But when you begin to see people change and become more comfortable with themselves, it begins to seem worth it all. And the greater the involvement, the greater the joy that is mutually shared.

The Pitfalls of Over-Involvement

There is, however, another side to involvement, a

more pessimistic side. There can be pitfalls as well as advantages to a close relationship with another person. Over-involvement, where one stays awake worrying about other people's problems or where one is unable to be emotionally detached once he is away from the problem, does nothing to help either person and can actually harm both.

Janelle was a girl who was usually on some kind of barbiturate or downer. She lived in a groggy, dimly-perceived world with an occasional change derived from an acid trip or an amphetamine. She was rarely herself—pretty, sweet, considerate Janelle.

At the height of my relationship with her, I suddenly became upset over the thought that someday she might overdose with pills and die. How would I take it? I did not know. One night in particular I was obsessed with my questions. I tossed and turned much of the night, wondering and praying that my question would never be put to the test.

The next day Janelle was still alive and still had the same problems. However, I was tired and unable to be of much help to her or anyone else. My over-involvement had lessened my effectiveness all around.

More recently I came closer to actually having my nightmare come true. John is an intelligent, popular tenth-grader who began coming in to talk. Wealthy, but neglected by his family, he pathetically reached out for anyone who would really care. Once when I merely said that I wished he would stop dropping pills every morning, he turned to me and said quietly, "You know, you're the only person who cares." Maybe his parents cared. But if they did, he needed to hear it.

Then, one day he dropped more than just one or two pills and came close to dying. It was not intentional. He simply forgot how many he had taken after the first few

87

took hold. He kept taking a few more and a few more until he lost consciousness.

Needless to say, I was upset and tried to find out what I could do to help. I looked at the past and saw things which could have been done differently. But I did not grovel in guilt feelings. I accepted the fact that I had not always acted or understood perfectly, but that, on the other hand, I had basically done a good job of relating to him. This time my energies were not dissipated in excessive heart-searching although, of course, emotion was present.

Sometimes over-involvement leads to an attempt to fit someone else into our mold. Here the Christian counselor seems particularly vulnerable. He often feels that his ideas and actions are right and expects the world to be able to see how right they are and copy them. This is, in effect, an attempt to monopolize another person for the adult's own ego-gratification. Some adults seem to function well only as the completely dominant authority figure, since, for various reasons involving their own low self-esteem, it gives them a sense of power and importance to manipulate other people. This is a role which is particularly easy for parents, teachers, counselors, and even ministers to fall into.

And, unfortunately, some young people, because of their own insecurities, want adults to tell them exactly what to do and then to commend them because they did the "right" thing. These teenagers seem to function well only as part of such overly dependent relationships. To allow them to do so is destructive, because part of the goal of good counseling is to enable people to learn enough self-confidence to function on their own. The really healthy person has close relationships with others but does not allow those relationships to obliterate his own identity.

On those occasions when the teenager himself desires the false security of being monopolized and dominated, there are simple ways of avoiding such over-involvement. For example, a girl who frequently came in to talk wanted to eat lunch with me at school. I avoided the added contact most days because she needed the lunch period to relate to her peers, just as I did. Yet I was careful not to appear rejecting. I simply was not available.

Another girl at the same school wanted me to make decisions for her because she did not want to be responsible for the results. Her parents and I had been trying to convince her that she should see a psychologist. One day, when she was taken to the hospital for an overdose, she decided she would make the appointment. Still very groggy from the effects of six downers, she asked me to call the therapist for her. She had a legitimate excuse— she was not sure she could make herself intelligible to anyone. However, I refused to call even though it would have been much easier all around. It was important that the responsibility for starting psychotherapy be hers, not mine.

More often than not, however, teenagers will resist a loss of their freedom. A Christian woman I know has a genuine concern for people and is sacrificial in her desire to help. But she can only relate to people from a position of dominance. Once when a young person disagreed with her on a choice of churches, she told the young boy that he had made his particular choice because of his poor spiritual condition. In actuality the church was biblical in stand and was a perfectly adequate choice. But it was his choice, not hers. In the end the boy had to decide between his spiritual freedom before God and his friendship with her. He chose to be free.

In a variety of ways Christians seem to be afraid to trust people to the divine leadership of the Holy Spirit. A number of colleges still require pledges from all their students, graduate included, that they will not dance, smoke, drink or attend the theater. Such a requirement could well indicate an over-involvement with the consciences of other people.

The Bible graphically portrays the Christian as related to Christ in much the same way as the human body functions in relationship to the brain. Christ directs each member. While it is true that certain principles of belief and behavior are clearly set forth in the Bible and a place is given for the authority of the local church, much in the way of decision making is left up to the individual as he is led by Christ. Yet parents, teachers, pastors and counselors often seem afraid to leave the young person to such divine guidance.

Parents whose children want to be teachers tell them to be doctors. In school, students are forced into chemistry when they want auto-shop or into art classes when they want math or biology. We decide they are stupid because of one bad test, which may only indicate that they were unprepared or sick or loaded on that day or that the test was too culturally influenced to be relevant to their ethnic background.

We push them toward prestigious colleges or toward Christian schools where their faith will be sheltered. We tell them they must believe that it is wrong to drink or smoke, or we go to the opposite extreme and insist that they exercise their Christian liberty in all matters. And all of this is just another way of being over-involved, this time with the personal consciences of the individuals we are trying to help.

The end result is frequently deceit. One girl who came from a strict religious background was forbidden to date or to wear skirts as short as fashion demanded a few years ago. Her solution was simple: She wore skirts and tops rather than dresses so that she could roll up the waist of the skirt on the way to school and unroll it on the way home. She could not date, but her parents never knew about all the necking that went on in secluded areas of the school grounds.

Sometimes, too, a situation develops where the young person is temporarily "used" by the helping adult. This usually happens when the counselor has suffered a loss in his personal life. For the interim, until his life adjusts, he may consciously or unconsciously attempt to fill the void with someone he is trying to help.

There are obvious reasons why this kind of relationship cannot endure. The adult's life will eventually even out and, since he will no longer need the young person in the same way, he will probably cut down the time spent together or even drop the teenager suddenly. The teenager will generally interpret this kind of action as further rejection. And rejection is not easily handled by a person with problems.

Then, too, when an individual makes a practice of allowing other people to become too dependent on him, and uses this dependence to gratify his own needs, he may soon find himself overwhelmed by too many demands. He has promised everything and now cannot fulfill these promises. His failure to live up to his commitments can only be interpreted as rejection by those he is trying to help.

Teachers, counselors and ministers in particular seem to have a need to prove that they can relate to the people they are trying to help. One young social worker drives his clients to wherever they need to go and personally provides housing for them. In a variety of small ways, he allows himself to be completely used because, in his case, he is afraid he is not helping them enough and he has a tremendous need to be needed. Then when people overwhelm him and he just cannot take all the pressure, he abruptly drops them. His clients are left wondering what they have done wrong.

Keeping Commitments

Commitments made to a person must be kept at all costs. That is why they must be wisely made to begin with. It is usually necessary to choose between many worthwhile tasks. Thus, we must decide to help where we think we can do the most good. Many times our unique relationship with a person, or the potential for that relationship, will be a determining factor.

One day I began to talk to a girl who had been on drugs—downers, grass, uppers. Then for a number of months she had put down, done well in a business course in school, and, in general, lived a happier life. But then the stresses began to build again.

She began dating a boy who dropped acid regularly. Furthermore, her home situation had gone from bad to worse. Her mother was deeply disturbed to the point where she did not care whether her children came home in time for dinner, after dinner or at all. Her stepfather wanted to marry Chris's younger fifteen-year-old sister. Her real father told Chris that unless she had sexual relations with boys, they would not like her.

Pressured by these circumstances, she began to drop acid along with her boy friend. Then, one night, she went to a party. She sat and observed, and what she saw disgusted her. Everyone freaking out, no one knowing or caring about reality. The scene was like a game of Russian Roulette played with high stakes. The next night was the same—and the next.

The following Monday, Chris came to see me. As she

put it, my caring had helped her put down before and she needed that help again. My relationship with her seemed to be unique in her experience. I cared and she apparently felt that no one else did. It was more important for me to help her than to become involved with someone totally new to me. In a sense I had made a prior commitment to Chris by having shown her a year ago that I cared enough to help. For that reason I set aside an hour a week to talk with her. By doing this, I committed myself to being available when she needed me and to helping her through her problems.

Dr. Viktor Frankl speaks similarly of the problem of conflicting obligations: "On a certain morning should I devote myself to my family or look up a patient in the hospital? Actually, there is no conflict when I can see that the value of my professional visit, in the service of mankind, is of a higher order than just sitting with my wife and daughter. But suppose my wife needs me because she is sick. Then, the choice seems to be one sick person against another. But there is a difference because in one case I am replaceable and in the other I am not. In the case of my patient at the hospital I can send a member of my staff to look after him. . . . If someone rings me up and wants an appointment with me, I first ask who recommended me as a doctor. If he says, 'A friend told me,' or 'Another doctor mentioned your name,' I am likely to refer him to a member of my staff. But when he says, 'I heard you speak on the radio ten years ago and I trust only you,' I'll make every effort to see him myself, even if he cannot pay a fee. For this is a unique obligation and I am relatively irreplaceable. . . . We have to see when we have a unique obligation and when we can be replaced by others."[11]

A few years ago a teenage friend of mine was arrested for drug abuse and then released on probation. Sometime in the middle of the night, my phone rang. After a night of hassling with the police and her parents, she called because she needed a safe sounding board where she could be herself. In desperation she asked me if I would help her put down. I thought quickly. Summer was coming and I would have more time. If the phone rang in the middle of the night, I could still sleep late the next morning. Yes, I could commit myself to helping her and could in all probability remain faithful to that commitment. Once I was in it, I continually let her know that the basic responsibility was hers. I could not and did not want to live her life for her. But I was morally obligated to keep my side of the bargain as she was obligated to keep her side.

Steering Clear of Manipulation

But if counselors and others who help, sometimes use the people they work with to satisfy their own needs, so also teenagers will sometimes to an even greater degree try to use the counselor. When I spend an hour on the phone in the middle of the night helping someone over the rough part of an LSD trip, I have to be careful not to allow myself to be manipulated into the position of making it easier for them to drop their next tab because I am there to hold their hand in the middle of the day or night.

In countless other ways teenagers and others will try to use the person counseling them. If the counselor is a teacher, they may expect a better grade. Some will try to demand time on a social level, too. This is fine except you can have only so many friends. In a school, students who are loaded will try to use the counselor or teacher as a hiding place until they come down. Or the counselor may be used as a protection from probation or jail.

Some manipulation, such as being used to hide some-

94

one from the police, is very obvious and inconsiderate. More subtle, and requiring more sensitivity in handling, is the kind of situation in which a student will try to replace a missing parent with the counselor. Again there is probably nothing wrong with this until it reaches the point when the helping adult tries to be a real parent to so many kids that he cannot handle it and starts to hurt people by rejection.

Typical of the need for a parent substitute is one sixteen-year-old girl who said: "I want to be with someone like you because I feel it has something to do with the pills and being alone. I am so damn sick of not having some kind of a mother. I just dream and wish that I lived with a person like you or _____, to be a mother who I could talk with."

When young people feel this way about me, it is a little frightening. I appreciate their sense of insecurity and I, too, wish they had a mother who cared. But I cannot become a mother to all those I meet who need it. Nor can I even start to develop an over-demanding relationship. To do so would be to become over-involved to the point where I would eventually have to pull back. Over-dependence for whatever motive will usually have a destructive rather than helpful effect.

Naturally when we help anyone there will be a certain amount of dependence. More with some; less with others. As a temporary state, this is therapeutic. But the counselor should be gradually moving the person nearer to self-dependence and dependence on God.

Over-involvement, whether it takes the form of being crushed by the problems of others or the form of trying to dominate the world around us, is not healthy for anyone. We cannot humanly carry all the problems of the world. Nor are we knowledgeable enough to take over the decision-making of others.

Avoiding the Messiah Complex

As I have tried to analyze the reasons for my over-involvement at times, I have concluded that for me and probably many others at the root is a distorted sense of guilt. Guilt because we are not always able to help someone sufficiently to our satisfaction. Guilt because we cannot help everyone we want to help. Guilt because we are not perfect.

Dr. Rollo May aptly calls this need for perfection the Messiah Complex. Dr. May explains: "... When the individual works with never relaxing tension, we become suspicious that the motive is his ego striving rather than the unselfish desire to contribute to humanity. ... It is the person's conviction of the indispensability of his own person, and the consequent feeling that his particular work is indispensable to humanity and the universe. Thus he is given a mask for his pride." He concludes this paragraph by reminding us that "the religious worker serves Christ: he is not Christ."[12]

Christ did not act as we so often tend to. Indispensable and active as He truly was, we do not read of His rushing around in ceaseless, nervous activity. Frequently in the gospels we read that He "went up in the hills to pray" or that He summoned certain ones, inviting them to come and join Him there. On at least one occasion He told His disciples, "Let's get away from the crowds for a while and rest."[13]

Christ's problem was not much different from ours. It was not easy to escape from the pressures around Him. People followed Him, the demands did not diminish. But with divine wisdom, Christ frequently attempted to get away and renew His spirit. He always showed divine detachment and balance—able to feel and care, yet not crushed by the multitudinous burdens of the crowds which so frequently surrounded Him.

And while Christ was directive in His teachings, He allowed people to lead their own lives. His motivation for helping them was never based on a cheap need to use them. When He healed the nobleman's son, for example, Christ did not ask for a financial payment from the father. He did not make an agreement with the family that they would join the local church or even follow His beliefs, nor did He demand any personal favors. Faith was all that was asked. But the result of Christ's healing activity was that not only did the father believe, but also "his whole house."[14]

However, a person who is aware of himself enough to recognize his tendency to become over-involved should not interpret all this as a sign of being a basically poor counselor. It may be a sign of a potentially good counselor. To have well-founded, strong ideas about life may be helpful when people ask you directly for advice, as long as you offer these ideas without rejecting their ideas or forcing yours on them. To feel personal gratification in our involvement with others is natural and good unless it becomes a more strongly motivating force than the good of the persons we are trying to help. And, above all, to feel deeply the problems of other people is the basis of a caring relationship. Gradually one learns to take the good part of his counseling relationships and shed the destructive part. He comes to understand the reasons for his over-involvement and is thus in a position to choose to act differently. And all the time he is seeking to be changed himself by the greatest counselor, the Holy Spirit.

The Counselor as God's Instrument

What God wants in each of us who desire to serve Him is an attitude of honesty concerning ourselves and others. Honesty to see our strengths as well as our weaknesses; honesty to see that to God we are a channel through whom He may help others. To be a channel through which God may work is the Christian's highest motivation.

When we are truly instruments usable by the Holy Spirit, we are able to accept ourselves for what we are, imperfect human beings. Such acceptance does not imply condoning sin or passivity. It does mean that while we constantly allow God to shape us closer and closer to the image of His Son, at the same time we accept our humanity and stop trying to prove ourselves. Rather than lowering our standards regarding what we expect from ourselves, our standards remain high. Realizing our humanity, we increasingly trust God to work through us. Thus the responsibility for results ultimately becomes His.

While it is easy to be self-protective and almost indifferent to the needs of others, it is also easy to let go and become too involved. But it is difficult to become balanced, combining involvement with a measure of emotional detachment. Yet that is what we must achieve if we are to be effective in helping others.

A teenager wrote the following words about a helpful adult. They beautifully sum up a constructive relationship between a parent, teacher, pastor or counselor and a young person. There is a completeness in the relationship—genuine warmth between the two, combined with wise detachment on the part of the adult.

"You didn't seem to do anything but be there. And yet a harbor doesn't do anything either, except to stand there with arms always outstretched, waiting for the traveler to come home."

In Summary

1. Humanly speaking, there is no way to change a

teenager's life except by a caring person's wholehearted and timely involvement with him.

2. All teenagers need empathetic adults who will stand with them in their pain and confusion and feelings of desperate loneliness.

3. Consistency is pivotal to whether or not adult involvement works, for to be under-involved shows a lack of caring while to be over-involved is to start something which cannot and should not be maintained if teenagers are to accept responsibility for themselves and for working toward solutions to their problems.

4. Involvement also means caring but not owning, suggesting, but not forcing, loving but not smothering, giving but not being walked over in return.

5. Involvement with teenagers cannot preclude your taking time to be *you*, to be with other adults, to be alone. If this posture is not accepted, physical and emotional exhaustion can actually harm what good work has been done.

chapter five

Building a Strong Counseling Relationship

Several months ago a fourteen-year-old boy came to me as a referral from the police. He had run away twice and more recently had been suspected of using drugs. Both of his parents hold moderately well-paying jobs in the community. Anxious, well-meaning, they say they will do anything to help their son.

Unfortunately for our relationship, however, Bruce did not choose to get counseling; he was forced into it. For a number of weeks we each endured the hour we spent together—Bruce describing how he repaired his motorcycle and what TV commercials were stupid and telling jokes while I listened. He was well aware of what he was doing. As he put it: "I have to be here and you have to listen, so let's make the best of it." But trust me? Never.

I eventually brought up subjects relating to school and

home, but I almost always got short answers which terminated any further discussion. I gave him some tests which showed he was bright but underachieving. He was pleased with the results, but still did not open up. I was careful not to have more contacts with the parents than necessary during this time, since the idea that I was telling them whatever Bruce said to me would be enough to prevent him from ever trusting me. And, as at least a temporary measure, I did all I could to be accepting and interested during the hours we spent, without pushing him to talk.

Then for about two minutes during an hour not long ago, he decided to level with me. In his mind the police had sent him to me so I could function as some kind of spy. He thought I would collect information about his use of drugs and his supplier and turn it over to the police. More than that, he felt that I would tell his parents his negative feelings about them. Then, as suddenly as he had opened up, he stopped talking. Again, I did not push. It was better to let him adjust to the trust that he had shown and then let him move at his own pace. I did tell him, however, that in view of his fears, I understood his reticence to talk and that all I really could do was promise him that he could trust me, that I would respect his confidence and try to be honest with him. I was not there as a spy. But when and if he decided to trust me was up to him.

The next week, for the first time, he talked seriously the whole hour. He had begun to trust.

The Need for Trust and Honesty

For Bruce, trust came slowly, partly because talking to me was not his idea in the first place. Some who are forced into counseling might never trust. Others who want help trust quickly. But if a person is to achieve the kind of involvement by which he will be able to change his view of himself, trust is a first, essential ingredient of that involvement. This is true not only in the counseling process but also in any adult-teenage relationships.

Trust develops on a firm, more lasting basis if it is founded on honesty. In a practical way, honesty demands that with few exceptions we do not trick people or go behind their backs.

When I was a teacher my students knew that I would "bust" them, openly, with their knowledge, if they *showed* me illegal drugs, if I *saw* them sell drugs or if they were so loaded that they could not handle themselves. They also knew that what they told me about themselves, as opposed to what I saw, would not be exposed. Because things were clearly spelled out, they felt safer in trusting. Therefore, on the few occasions when it was necessary for me to turn someone in to the authorities, that act did not terminate any relationships.

Several people suggested that I preserve my counseling relationship at school by telling other teachers what I saw and by letting them turn students in when that was required. I could not personally agree with this plan because it obviously betrayed the students' trust.

Once a reputation for trust is established, half the battle in relating to teenagers is won. However, trust is so vital to most young people that it is frequently tested and retested. When a teenager with whom I have had a good relationship suddenly avoids me or talks in vague generalities, I can assume that something has gone wrong in the trust that exists between us. Sometimes he is doing something which is generally unacceptable, such as going back on drugs, and is afraid of rejection. Or I may have done something, or he may think I have done something, which has come through to him as rejection.

Gossip, even when unfounded, can hurt a relationship, particularly when one deals with groups of people. A student who tells me that she slept with her boyfriend on Saturday night may also have told her girl friend. If, through the girl friend, whom I also know, the word gets around, the person may blame me until the problem can be talked out. Usually I find that the best approach in handling such problems is to honestly ask the teenager what is wrong. If he does not want to talk about it, I do not push. I wait. I am available when he does want to talk.

Sharing Sorrows and Joys

Once a strong element of trust has been established between two people, a good therapeutic relationship can be built.

Of those factors which go into building a good relationship, empathy is one of the most important. Psychologist Dr. Rollo May, in his book *The Art of Counseling*, gives a definitive example of empathy when he relates his feelings as he talks with a student.

"As a counselor I had become so absorbed in his story that his emotions had become my emotions. His feeling of desperation as he struggled through high school, his realization of the loneliness of existence and the harshness of destiny, became my own experience, felt on my pulse as they had originally been on his. And when he concluded by stating his determination to stick it out at college if it killed him, I felt a certain exhilaration as though this resolution had been made by my own will. This partial identification was so real that if I had spoken aloud my voice would no doubt have partaken of the hesitant, quavering quality of his. The conclusion is forced upon us that the ego or psychic state of the counselor had temporarily become merged with that of the counselee; he and I were one psychic unity."[1]

The apostle Paul stated the same concept: "When others are happy, be happy with them. If they are sad, share their sorrow."[2] Paul often showed this kind of relationship with the various churches with which he was in contact. In Corinth, he once postponed a visit because if he had gone he would have had to correct them and their sadness would have made him sad. In a letter to the Corinthians he further explained: "I did not want to come to you and be made sad by the very people who should make me glad. For I am convinced that when I am happy, then you too are happy."[3]

Such empathy is also shown in the life of Christ when He changed the water to wine and then took part in the bridal festivities, as well as when He wept with Martha at the tomb of her brother Lazarus.

Because empathy is so vital in any helping relationships, it must be real. Teenagers are quick to spot phoniness of any kind. True empathy does not mean that we must have experienced everything. One does not have to be an unwed mother to understand unwed mothers, nor does one have to be an addict to help addicts. But empathy does mean that we attempt to put ourselves in the place of the person to whom we are relating.

With a person with a drug problem, for example, I freely admit that I have never smoked pot or dropped acid. However, I have lived long enough to feel pain, both physical and mental, and so I can appreciate their discomfort even though it may come from a different source than mine.

An old Indian proverb says, "Grant that I may not criticize my neighbor until I have walked a mile in his moccasins." Perhaps the following narrative by a fifteen-year-old girl illustrates what this kind of empathy may mean:

"It had been pouring. The howling wind and the icy water splattered on top of me through the broken glass. It was freezing, my teeth were chattering.

"Reach for the blanket, I remember it has been stolen. I crawl to the floor. It's cold too. I pull on my sweat shirt, I brush a moth off. I reach for a box and tear it apart. I try to block the wind and water with it. It comes off.

"The street lights are dimly visible. Some trash cans are turned over by the wind. Trash is all over the street. Also the added privilege of flying saucers, better known as trash can lids. All this blends with the gray brown buildings, the fire escape, and the empty street.

"My so-called father is in the kitchen. There is no light. We can't afford it, not with him drinking like he does. The stale smell of his cigarette is all over the house. He's been at it for hours.

"My mother gets up. Her face is dull, wrinkled and dirty. She passes her hand through her knotty, un-combed long hair. She walks over to the greasy stove, turns on the knob, the gas has been disconnected. She screams. He yells. Now we can't even have reheated coffee. He walks out. A rat runs by. She kicks it. I slouch myself on the bare mattress. She yells at me. I can't take it, walk out. She throws a beer can at me, cursing.

"Dope? Drugs? Will it help me forget? Will it be better? Why not?"

When we lack the human capacity to feel what another person is experiencing, we can make up for it by the power of Christ's life in us; for as Christ is allowed to live His life through us, we show His divine capacity for caring and feeling for others. This is the truest cure for phoniness.

Sympathy Is Not Empathy

Empathy involves caring, not mere sympathizing.

Sympathy is sentiment and can be weakening. Statements like, "You poor thing, how can you endure it?" or "I don't blame you for anything after all you've been through," can make a person feel so hopeless and sorry for himself that he will give up trying to change and will be consumed by feelings of self-pity. I have seen teenagers receive counseling which blamed their drug habit on parents and environment to the point where the students gave up and decided they were doomed to drug abuse. After all, how could anyone with such a bad background ever rise out of it.

One young girl continually tells me that she cannot put down. Every time she tries, she is besieged by friends who try to offer her a few pills, a drag of marijuana—anything which will pull her down to their level again. Her trouble is she wants those pills. For me to offer sympathy and pity, whether in word or by facial expression or tone of voice, would be destructive. And many times I want to sympathize. I want to let her know what a rotten deal I think she has had in life so far, how unthinkingly destructive her parents are, how sorry I am that she suffers so much more than most people. But all this would only add to her feelings of helplessness.

Real empathy means identifying with the other person in a way that becomes strengthening. If I can show her that I understand the strong feelings and desires that she has, and if I can go on to assure her that, difficult as it will be, she can overcome the habit, then I will be empathizing with her. Empathy means saying: "I understand your feeling that you can't stop taking drugs. I agree that you have had a lot of bad breaks in life. But you can make it. It will be difficult, but possible, and at least now you won't be alone because you have people who know what you're going through, who will stick by you and care." Empathy means understanding and accepting the hurt feelings, being able to feel them your-self, but not wallowing in them.

The result should be strength, not weakness. The person should feel stronger because someone really does understand and yet feels there is hope. If the counselor only sympathizes, the counselee is likely to feel that now that the counselor has a better grasp of the problem, he, too, agrees that it is terrible and hopeless.

Expressing Acceptance

A truly empathetic relationship will also be an accepting relationship. Acceptance does not mean we must like everything someone is doing. Many of the people I talk to have morals and values which clash violently with my own. Acceptance means that while we may reject certain actions performed by an individual, we do not reject the individual.

One of the major problems confronting young people as they graduate from high school is whether or not to live with someone of the opposite sex. Last summer I spent hours talking with several different girls who were each trying to decide between living alone or with a boy whom they really loved. The decisions were agonizing —they were each in love, came from a lonely, rejecting family background and wanted to feel close to another human being. All of them had been brought up to believe that sex outside of marriage is wrong, and so there was tremendous conflict.

As I talked with them, I had to, in all honesty, say, "Even apart from any spiritual values, which you may or may not consider important, I believe that there are tremendous psychological problems in living with a man outside of marriage. One of the main problems, as I see it, is that to you, a woman, sex means caring and permanence. It means he loves you now and he intends to keep loving you. If he does not see it that way, you may experience great feelings of rejection—which are the opposite of what you need right now."

I had to be honest. Yet as I saw two of the girls moving in the direction of living with their boyfriends, it was equally important for me to show my acceptance of them as people: "I like you, I care about you and no matter what you decide, those feelings will not be altered." And one of the greatest compliments I have received came from the girl who said in reply: "I know that. I know that I can tell you what I'm doing even when you don't approve, and you won't reject me as a person."

Conversely, one of the most uncomplimentary events which has happened to me was when another girl sneaked off to move in with her boyfriend and to this day has never told me. Obviously my acceptance of her did not reach over to her in a strong enough way, for in the end she could not trust me to really accept her as she was.

People should not have to buy our acceptance by fitting into our mold. One boy I know has taken every illegal drug available, including heroin. He has been in repeated trouble with the police and his sexual life would shock many. Yet, he has made a great effort during this past year to change his life and to try to succeed in school. Considering his background and the nature of his problems, he is trying harder and succeeding more than most of us. For his determination and guts I respect him. He has an outlook of optimism and a drive to succeed that makes him an admirable person whom I can readily accept. But I do not always like what he does, nor do I hesitate to openly disagree with him. Our relationship is strong enough for him not to interpret my disagreement as rejection.

Practicing Openness

Openness in stating our beliefs and feelings is important in helping teenagers. When we talk with them, we should make it plain that we intend to be honest, and that we expect the same from them. This means admitting when we are wrong and letting them say what they wish to say—without becoming angry or rejecting.

Such openness requires patience and practice. Allowing someone to be open with us means hearing some things we would rather not hear. It requires learning to separate emotionally what a person does and says from what he is and can become.

I know a lonely young girl who sleeps in anyone's bed she can find. But first I saw her two years earlier trying to make her parents notice her and love her. I know a young man who feels there is no moral code in the universe and that people should base their sex life upon the casualness which they observe in the animal world. Yet he has spent a good deal of his life living in the back seat of a car, along with several brothers and sisters, as his parents roamed around the country with no home, not even a motel room at times. When either of these students levels about his or her life, what is said is bound to be shocking and objectionable to most of us. But if we are to reach today's young people, we must become more shockproof. We need not always accept their behavior, nor shed our own personal standards of conduct, but we must be able to hear things we are not used to hearing and be able to see beyond the behavior to the tremendous worth of the individual.

Openness requires a certain personal toughness in the adult, not only because he will hear unpleasant things if people really feel they can be honest with him, but because he himself will sooner or later be attacked. Among other things, I have been accused of sexual promiscuity

110

and of smoking marijuana. I made one boy furious because I was instrumental in preventing him from committing suicide, and it took another boy a long time to adjust to me because I refused to agree that he should be institutionalized.

I do not like being the object of someone's anger, nor do I enjoy having my personal life attacked and distorted. And for each of us, our own sensitive areas or weak spots hurt the most if the young person we are helping hits near them. Yet such attacks will come if our counseling relationships are open.

The attacks will occur at times because the person is angry and lashing out, much as we all do to a lesser degree when we have a hard day at work and come home and snap at various members of our family. At other times, they will be the teenager's way of testing us. A teenager will try to make us reject him so that he can prove he really is rejectable; or conversely, he will try to make us reject him so that if we do not, he will have the extra reinforcement of knowing we really must care if we still like him after all he has said and done. Such tests vary greatly. One girl called me in the middle of the night to see if that would make me give up on her. Others tell me some "shocking" fact about themselves or criticize me for something.

Whatever the test, it is vital to avoid rejecting an individual as a person. We can refuse to accept criticism if it is unwarranted, we can quietly but firmly discuss reasons why they should not call in the middle of the night unless they really need us, but we must have enough control and emotional detachment to remain accepting so that they can remain open. If the counselor cannot handle his own feelings, then he should seek help for himself, but he must not allow his own feelings of inadequacy to affect his counseling relationships.

Likewise we need to be careful of certain things in our openness with the counselee. While we should not be dishonest, we need to be cautious when we confront a teenager with something which will disturb him. Is he ready to take it? Is our relationship strong enough, or will he reject us for having been so blunt? The degree of open confrontation which the young person will be able to handle depends on how strong he is, how accepting of him we are and how intense his relationship with us is.

When I was teaching in the public school system, a girl who had slowly begun to trust me became involved with the police in a narcotics incident. Because her problem had become apparent and her position at school had become tenuous, her parents were anxious to obtain outside help. But the girl had a built-in distrust of psychologists and resisted any kind of suggestions her parents made. Because she had a relatively good relationship with me, I was finally able to convince her that she should accept professional help. She did not reject me for telling her what she needed because she already was fairly sure of my acceptance.

When we accept a person as a whole person, we can at times confront him with his needs without breaking the relationship. Actually such confrontation will frequently strengthen the relationship. For one thing, it shows the person that we really do know him quite well and still accept him. It shows that we are willing to risk his anger and make ourselves uncomfortable in order to help.

Some time ago, a young boy at my school became difficult for anyone to get along with. Usually amiable and pleasant, he had now become quite the reverse. In the course of a day or two, the gist of his story came out: a mother telling him he was dumb, a father spending far more time with an older brother, failing grades at school. Particularly strong were his feelings of rejection from the father. As gently as I could, I told him he was not his usual agreeable self and I asked him if he thought it was possible that perhaps he was taking out his anger for his father on us at school. He agreed, and with that awareness his disposition improved. Now and then he lapsed into belligerence, but it did not last because we could honestly talk about the why of what he was doing and he trusted me more than before. Not only did his behavior improve, but we became closer and I could help him better. He opened up more when he had problems instead of bottling up his feelings.

The Art of Listening

While empathy and acceptance are ingredients of a good relationship, listening is one vehicle through which these characteristics may be shown. Many of us are willing to attend extra church services and to engage in many church activities, but we only grudgingly give time to listening to someone talk about a problem. Listening sounds so passive, so lacking in excitement and glamour. But if there is one thing teenagers want today, it is to be heard, and for the most part the adult world is too busy to stop and listen. Unless we take the time, we will be unable to form the kind of relationship with teenagers which will in any way reach them.

To listen means, first of all, to offer the gift of ourselves. It means turning off the TV or missing a few hours of sleep to listen to someone. Few things we can do in life imply caring and loving more than the almost lost art of listening. We give money, which in our affluence is not always too hard, but so infrequently do we give our time to listen, nor do we always know how.

Real listening means to really stop talking until we

have heard the person out. Particularly when someone is angry, the best procedure in helping him is to let him vent his feelings thoroughly before working out constructive solutions. Even when a person stops talking in a spontaneous way, he may have more to say which may be brought out by some gentle encouragement—but not probing.

Last week I talked to a young college man about his problems with the girl he wants to marry. He described his strong positive feelings for her, but then he hesitated and stopped. To help him get more of his feelings out, I asked him if he could describe more fully his reticence about something concerning her. Because he was close to telling me anyway, he went on to describe his fear of being hurt by women as he had been hurt in the past and as his father had been hurt. Because I already knew from the girl friend that he was also having some specific sexual conflicts regarding her, I knew that he had not told me everything that was bothering him. But usually what will not come out with gentle probing is better left until the person feels more confidence in talking. Therefore, I did not try to make him tell more, but rather offered some constructive suggestions as to how he could solve some of the problems he had brought up. I listened to all he was willing to say—no more, no less.

We lecture, issue commands and lay down rules, but do we listen and find out what young people are thinking? Time after time, I have heard teenagers express a desire to talk to their parents if they would only stop and listen. Some actually come in to talk about how they can work out the lines of communication between themselves and their parents. To me, that is pathetic. They want to discuss how to talk to those who should be closest to them.

For parents or counselors to listen to children and

young adults does not usually require special technique, but it does demand keeping quiet until the young person's feelings become clear. It demands detachment, not saying, "How could you do this to me?" or "I didn't raise you to turn out like this." Instead we must forget, for the moment, our guilt, our failure, all that threatens us, and try to listen to them—and watch for clues to their feelings for us.

A boy who relates poorly to his father tried to talk to him and got grounded. Then, because he was afraid to try to talk again, he made him a gift. What he was trying to say was, "I'm confused. We don't understand each other, but I love you." But so far the message has not come through to the father. He is too busy looking at low grades to hear and feel what his son is trying to say.

The other day the boy told me he wanted to commit a deed of vandalism in order to get his father's attention and to hurt him. If he does destroy property or steal a car and ends up in Juvenile Hall, his father will be the first to say, "I don't understand. I've given him all he needs and wants."

At times I have talked to someone who had a problem for which there was no real solution. I had no advice to give. Yet he felt better just from having expressed his feelings and from knowing someone cared enough to listen.

Many problems that are presented to a counselor have concrete solutions. I can give advice on college entrance requirements, abortions, communication problems between people, religious conflicts, ethical and moral problems. I can send a student with VD to a free clinic or give intelligence testing to a potential college student.

But, more often people feel alone, depressed, afraid, in need of human contact. They want someone to care while they slowly and painfully work out more subtle problems. And part of caring is listening. So for such people, indeed for most people who have problems, listening is at least as important as any well-founded advice we may offer.

A while back an elderly, retired woman came to my office just once. She had decided to stop blaming herself for past failure and to create a new life for herself. She would cultivate new friendships, she said, and start taking time to do things for her own pleasure instead of her children's well-being. For most of the hour that she spent with me, she poured out her feelings and cried. At the end of the hour she left, claiming that she had been greatly helped, when all I had really done was listen and give some support to her feelings of taking a more positive view of herself. Months later I heard from her and things were still going well. She was not a person who needed any long-range counseling, so in her case one afternoon of understanding and listening was all that was needed to help her make a more fulfilling life for herself.

A teenager who sensed her need for someone who would hear her, wrote this question which sums up the human need for someone to listen:

What if I had a problem?
Could I talk to you?
Even if it was something
    you couldn't understand?
Could I tell you my problems
    of sex or parents or God?
Would you listen?

And, then, to answer her own question after finding someone she could talk to:

I sat in the middle of my mind today,

116

I had to figure out my head.
I wanted you to know
   because you'll listen to me.
You'll listen—and you won't condemn.
My head is swimming around in confusion.
Who is God ... Why do we cry ...
   What is love ... How can we know?
You can always help me
   by being around ... and you are.
You're easy to be with,
I can talk at my own speed.

The Miracle of Transformation

A relationship like this between an adult—pastor, teacher, parent, counselor—and a teenager takes a lot of time to work out. But in such a relationship which is honest, empathetic, accepting and open—where two people care about, respect, understand and appreciate each other—miracles can happen.

Dr. Rollo May says of the appreciation in such a relationship: "... It raises the prestige of the one who is understood, and helps give him a sense of worth as a person. This understanding breaks down the barriers which separate a man from his fellows, it draws the other human being for a moment out of the loneliness of his individual existence and welcomes him into community with another soul. It is like inviting the traveler in from his snowy and chilly journey to warm himself for an hour before the fire on another's hearth. Such understanding, it is not too much to say, is the most objective form of love. That is why there is always a tendency on the part of the counselee to feel some love toward the counselor, this person 'who understands me.' There are few gifts that one person can give to another in this world as rich as understanding."[4]

117

The results of such a relationship can be profound in the changing of a human personality. Yet even when a counselor has had extensive training and experience and uses his skills to their greatest advantage, he cannot say, "This person I totally understand and therefore can cure." The counseling relationship is too complicated for that because man himself is complicated. The psalmist was indeed right when he said, "I am fearfully and wonderfully made."[5]

And it is the therapist with the finest skills who will have the objectivity and humility to agree with Dr. May's statement, "Finally, after all our discussion, we come to the realization that there is a great area in the transformation of personality which we do not understand, and which we can attribute only to the mysterious creativity of life. . . . As the motto has it, 'The physician furnishes the conditions—God works the cure.' Like the doctor, we may bind up the wound; but there are all the forces of life welling up in their incalculable spontaneity in the growing together of skin and nerve tissues and the reflowing of blood to perform the healing. Before the creative forces of life, the true counselor stands humbly. And his humility is not of the false sort, for the deeper his understanding of personality the more clearly he realizes how minute his efforts in comparison to the greatness of the whole. He says with the psalmist, 'Lord, this is too wonderful for me.' I am myself frank to say that when the limits of my own understanding are reached, I understand the miracle of the transformation of personality in terms of that age-old but ever-new concept, the grace of God."[6]

In Summary

1. Trust is the chief ingredient in the establishment of a good relationship with a teenager.

2. Teens need empathy which understands and encourages growth, not sympathy which fosters self-pity.

3. Trust and empathy do not mean approval of a person's actions but honest acceptance and caring for the person whether he or she fits our mold or not.

4. Openness should be two-sided: The adult point of view has a right to be presented as well as the teenage view, and neither should feel put down or rejected for what they believe.

chapter six

Guidelines for Therapy in Groups

"I hate her!" "That class is like a concentration camp!" "Do you suppose she's always been like this?" "Maybe she's just had a rough life." "Well, she really isn't too bad as a person."

Such were the comments which arose from a discussion group of about thirty teenagers, most of whom had just been in the class of the most unpopular teacher in the school.

At first, they were quiet, unresponsive, almost frightened. Then I set down the basic guidelines for our discussion: "We have the right to disagree with each other—teacher to student, student to teacher and student to student. But we do not have the right to ridicule or put each other down for having differing viewpoints."

After being handed that rather broad gesture of freedom, the students at first looked a little startled and unsure. Then the braver ones launched out into what became a hostile tirade against their former teacher. One by one the others joined in. Ordinarily, I would have disliked a prolonged discussion of a fellow colleague, but this time to stifle such expression of feeling would have been to allow the emotions to build, possibly into eventual destructive action.

And in the course of an hour, the feelings were let out, diluted in intensity, and turned from hate into an attempt to feel for and understand the teacher involved. Such a quick transition from hate to understanding would have been difficult to achieve in individual counseling. But with the strength and security and the interplay of ideas which exist in a group, most of the thirty teenagers present were able to work satisfactorily through some strong unpleasant feelings.

Alienation: An Increasing Threat

Since the beginning of time, people have needed the security of groups as well as separate, individual friendships. This need is stronger than ever today when alienation from others seems to be an increasing threat.

In his book *Future Shock*, Alvin Toffler says: ". . . we form limited involvement relationships with most of the people around us. Consciously or not, we define our relationships with most people in functional terms. So long as we do not become involved with the shoe saleman's problems at home, or his more general hopes, dreams and frustrations, he is, for us, fully interchangeable with any other salesman of equal competence. . . . We have created the disposable person. . . ."[1]

While Toffler points out good and bad aspects of our society's trend to develop limited involvements, I see in what he has described in phrases such as "disposable person," "Monday-to-Friday Friends," and "Rent-a-Person" a terrible alienation and aloneness which is at the root of many adolescent problems.

Toffler goes on: "Combine this with the accelerated through-put of places and things, as well as people, and

122

we begin to glimpse the complexity of the coping behavior that we demand of people today. Certainly, the logical end of the direction in which we are now traveling is a society based on a system of temporary encounters, and a distinctly new morality founded on the belief, so succinctly expressed by the co-ed in Fort Lauderdale, that 'frankly, you'll never see these people again.' "[2]

The Functions of Group Counseling

A sense of community. To counteract the alienation of our time, many people are becoming involved in group counseling sessions. Here for the first time some find the kind of closeness and community that is lacking in their lives.

In one group which I conducted, a young boy came who had been completely rejected by his peers up to that time in his life, a rejection that had been overt in its manifestations. Other children had forced Jerry to carry their books, run errands for them and perform ridiculous things like "jump six times" or "bark like a dog." As he became older, the rejection was more subtle, but effective, and the more he was rejected, the more rejectable he became. He wore dirty clothes, withdrew into himself, never talked and was known throughout the school as a classroom discipline problem.

Then as he became involved in this group and became brave enough to talk and interact, other teenagers began to accept him in a genuine way, and for the first time I could remember, I saw Jerry smile.

One day he could honestly say to the group, "I feel that you really accept me." Not long after that, the others started to include him in some of their social activities. Jerry was no longer alone because within a group he learned some self-acceptance as a result of the group's acceptance of him.

123

It is this group acceptance and its effect on an individual's feelings of alienation and aloneness which make group counseling such a vital tool. As those of us who have worked in churches, schools and universities are acutely aware, there do not seem to be enough of us to reach all students individually in an age when they need us more than ever. For this reason, as well as for its effectiveness, I have found group counseling helpful in building meaningful relationships with teenagers.

Dr. Herbert Gerjuoy, a psychologist on the staff of the Human Resources Research Organization, argues that if we bring a person "together with others who are moving through the same experience, people he can identify with and respect, we strengthen him. The members of the group come to share, even if briefly, some sense of identity. They see their problems more objectively. They trade useful ideas and insights. Most important, they suggest future alternatives for one another."[3]

Thus, relationships between teenagers will often in themselves effect change. To begin with, many times young people will more quickly take criticism and suggestions from each other than from an adult. For example, at one time, the students in our school were concerned about cafeteria food. Some wanted to use a boycott to show their protest. Others, however, wanted to walk off grounds, which was against school rules. The subject came up in a class discussion. Rather than tell them that a legal boycott was a better solution than an illegal walk-out, it was better to let them arrive at their own resolution. I could ask objective questions such as, "What will you ultimately accomplish with each method?" or "What possible problems will arise?" or "What image of teenagers do you wish to create?" But in the end, they opposed an illegal method with their own arguments. They sufficiently convinced each other not to break the rules to the point where there was nothing more than a quiet, well-ordered and highly effective boycott. Throughout the school, in various discussion groups, both formal and informal, the students influenced each other with results which never could have been achieved by adult orders.

Self-esteem. Often, too, the group interaction will have a dramatic effect on the self-esteem of a teenager, particularly since at that age peer recognition is of such vital importance. In individual counseling, the young person can say to me, as one young man did, "You accept me, but you're an adult." But in a group, peer acceptance can be dramatically effective in changing behavior and increasing self-esteem.

A fifteen-year-old girl who transferred from another school at mid-semester immediately became a strongly disruptive force in the class. At impulse, she would get up, wander around the room, walk over to a boy she hardly knew and ask him home for dinner or insult someone's way of dress. My amazement at her behavior was great, but no greater than that of the class in general.

Then, quietly, intuitively, with almost no planning, we all did the same thing. We ignored every bizarre, ridiculous thing she did and pulled together more tightly as a group. In her isolation, she began to realize that the behavior which had previously never failed to bring her a lot of attention was getting her nowhere. Then once in a while she would do something helpful or considerate. She would say something constructive in a discussion; she would complete her assignment; she would politely respond to another student. Each time we would all immediately accept her—tell her what she had done was good, comment on her new dress and in general treat her like any other teenager.

The boys in the class were particularly helpful because they were the ones she was most anxious to get attention from. In just a few weeks her behavior was almost as acceptable as any other teenager because this time her good behavior, not the bad, had won her the attention she wanted so much. And, above all, much of that attention had come from her own peers.

Furthermore, in a group, there is the strength that comes from knowing other people have the same problems. A new perspective can be gained from hearing other people's reactions.

Trust. Finally, within the acceptance and support of a group, there can be the development of an attitude of trust for the adult leading the group, and problems can be solved using both individual and group methods as adjuncts to each other.

A young girl once expressed this view of life while she was a member of a group of teenagers: "My philosophy of life is death. I regard death as the ultimate escape. But I also respect death. Shouldn't it be used only under the most strenuous of conditions? . . . It is said, I have to back up my opinions with facts. Are the scars on my wrists and arms enough facts? Or will my philosophy of life only be proved and believed at my funeral?

"Perhaps that is not my philosophy of life. Perhaps it is escape, and death is the final escape. Maybe I shun responsibility; maybe I'm tired of the screwed world. . . . How do I escape? Sometimes I'll go for a long walk in the hills surrounding my home and escape from the busyness of the world. Sometimes I'll slash my wrists or arms and escape with my blood. Sometimes I'll drop a few pills and mentally escape; alcohol is pretty good for that, too."

I did not know Julie in a one-to-one relationship, but the views which she had on life gave me a pretty clear picture of a disturbed teenager. Yet outwardly she appeared poised, bright, attractive, well-adjusted. And each time that we encountered each other in the group I knew that if I were to help her, she would first have to reach out and ask.

She watched as I responded in discussions which ranged in topics from getting along with teachers to dying in a war. She saw some teenagers show trust by telling me things young people do not ordinarily tell an adult like what last Saturday's party was like or how "unfair" a school rule was. And still I only knew her in a group.

Then a death occurred in her family—suddenly and uniquely tragic. And Julie ended up in my office, hysterical, wanting to slash her wrists.

I was there all along. But she only found me and trusted me when she was in desperate need, and then only because she had first learned to know me in the safety of a group.

Guidelines for Group Counseling

Group counseling, like individual counseling, must include sensitive, intuitive actions and reactions on the part of the counselor. There are no rules or instructions for each case that comes along. But there are some guidelines which, if loosely followed, may be helpful.

Establishing trust between counselor and group members. As in individual counseling, the first absolute essential in working with a group is the establishing of a trusting relationship between the counselor and the group members. Unless young people feel that they can trust the counselor and that he cares about them, he is doomed to failure. To build trust is not easy and it takes time.

The first day in one group, a girl walked in bristling with anger, obviously showing her contempt. Later she told me that a girl friend had hated the discussion because I had offended her by condemning the use of drugs. It took some control and patience to work out a relationship with a girl already determined to resist that relationship. But by my not turning off at her hostility and my accepting her, particularly by drawing her into group discussions, we actually became good friends. In many situations, trust can be fostered in groups more quickly than in individual contacts. For in the group a person feels protected by the presence of his friends. If the adult does reject him, at least his friends may give him their support.

In a group, as with individuals, trust is fostered through such qualities as acceptance, honesty and caring: acceptance of others no matter what they say, although not necessarily agreeing; honesty with oneself first and then with others; caring, without which there is no real counseling process. All of this does not mean that the counselor may not have his own hang-ups, but it does mean that those hang-ups cannot interfere in his relationships with others.

Establishing trust among group members. It is also essential that members of a group trust each other. One girl in a group, who usually talks a lot, suddenly became quiet during almost one whole group session. When she did talk, it was in vague, safe generalities.

Finally, the problem came out. She did not trust a new boy in the group because he knew her sister and she was afraid that what she said would get back to her family. Finally, she confronted him with her problem. Not only was he able to assure her that he could keep quiet, but she gave him the same promise not to repeat what was said in the group.

Keeping confidences. The whole problem of not repeating what teenagers say in groups is vital to the success of group counseling. Between the counselor and teenagers the problem of keeping confidences is particularly touchy if the teenagers feel that the counselor is likely to repeat information to a probation officer, parents or school administrators. In a similar way, young people must feel free to criticize institutions such as the church or school in which they function. By so doing they can often be made to feel more understanding toward the adult authority structure.

Using roleplay. A careful use of roleplaying can sometimes achieve this end. When I have been in discussions where teenagers criticize a teacher, for example, because he turned in a student who was too stoned to even sit in his chair without falling, I have set up a roleplaying situation where the students play the parts of the student, teacher and perhaps parents and administrator. All of a sudden the students feel the pressure that the teacher is under or the frustration and anxiety which the parents feel. And such feelings begin to bridge the gap of understanding between youth and adults.

Roleplaying can bring about understanding within the church or with the police, too. But it must be used carefully, depending on the openness of the counselor and students, so that the results will not be damaging. For example, such problems as unwanted pregnancies, abortions or other guilt-generating issues could, in a roleplaying situation, bring out stronger feelings than the counselor is able to cope with. People should only be opened up to the degree that they can then be put back together. They should never be cracked open and then left that way. Ideally, it is good for self-esteem to be strengthened first before the person begins to face things about himself that are painful to look at.

As in individual counseling, trust is therefore a key word in group counseling—trust for the therapist and in each other, and ultimately self-trust and the ability to bring out problems which are painful and need solutions.

Problems Inherent in Group Counseling

Like any useful counseling technique, group counseling has its problems as well as its assets.

Pretense. O. Hobart Mowrer, in his book *The New Group Therapy*, says that even when we do meet in groups together we put on a phony front. We pretend to be perfect and feel alone and defensive because we know we are not perfect. "We dare not be sinners. Many Christians are unthinkably horrified when a real sinner is suddenly discovered among the righteous. So we remain alone with our sin, living in lies and hypocrisy."[4]

In a group where such a front exists, a counselor can point out gently but directly the hesitancy to be honest with each other. Members of the group may be afraid to be honest—afraid that others will reject them or that they will come out looking worse than the rest of the group.

The counselor can encourage some of the group to open up at least a little. He must, of course, be careful to be accepting of those people who begin to talk. Once started, however, the group will usually begin to support and encourage each other, and they will become increasingly open in sharing their problems. The counselor serves as a catalyst to start the process going.

Group size. Another problem in group counseling is determining the optimum number of people to be included in a particular group. If the group is too large, it is sometimes difficult to identify problems quickly. Even in a normal-sized group, it is difficult. One boy in a rather large group withdrew and became quiet. Because of the size of the group, it was easy to ignore him and relate only to the rest of the group. Then one day after the session, I noticed that he seemed quite upset. Although I usually wait for a person to approach me with a problem, this time, because it seemed that the problem had arisen during the discussion, I made the first move and told him he could feel free to come in and talk if something had upset him. It is essential that a counselor exercise care that no person leave a group deeply upset.

Later he came in. He said he hated the group and wanted to get out of it. I made no emotional response but asked him to tell me more about his feelings. As he spoke, his hostility subsided considerably and he frankly admitted the real problem: his shyness with others of his age, which, of course, made a group discussion painful at times, combined with an infatuation over a girl who usually sat next to him. We talked the problem out somewhat, but arrived at no quick, easy answers. But since then, he has seemed a little more relaxed and perhaps has realized that one way to learn to be comfortable in groups is to be in those groups. Most important to me is the fact that our relationship did not deteriorate because of his outburst, but, if anything, was strengthened.

Conversely, a group can also be a vehicle through which problems can be seen in a different light. A girl whom I had seen privately for about four weeks joined a group and became friends with another girl her age. I had earlier picked up feelings of deep distrust from my patient—suspicions that people watched her and followed her. But one afternoon when the two girls walked home together, her fear of this unknown person who was supposed to be following her came out with deep intensity. The incident scared the second girl, who then told me. Similar insights can come from just watching and listening to the conversations within the group.

Anonymity. Yet for all of the information the counselor can gain from young people in group counseling, he must be continuously on guard against allowing the problems of one individual to be hidden or even made worse because he becomes an anonymous, quiet member of a more talkative group. For in nonhomogeneous groups, there will be vast differences between the members. Often these differences are helpful. Quiet people may be encouraged to talk by someone less fearful of rejection. People who live only by subjective feelings may gain a balance by contact with the more objective members of the group, and vice versa. But sometimes these differences aggravate individual problems and some members of the group may take advantage of the lack of unity. Thus, it is important for the counselor to intuitively feel his way into setting up a group which will be of mutual benefit to its members.

Involvement without follow-through. Another danger in group counseling, which also relates to groups which are too large, is the encouragement of involvement without sufficient follow-through. When the original relationship is fostered, people should feel free to approach the counselor if a personal need for this arises. And some things should be discussed privately. No one should be forced to discuss anything in a group which he would prefer to discuss in private. Therefore, a counselor with a group should make sure he has time to accommodate the individual needs of that group. Otherwise, there is a certain unfairness in encouraging such involvement.

Often very specific needs which require individual attention are precipitated through group work. For example, in our discussions on drugs, one girl raised the common problem of how to handle a boyfriend who was on drugs. Eventually, she wanted to talk alone because the problem was in truth much deeper. She, too, had tried drugs but had put down. The boy was taking speed and used it as a weapon by saying that he would take it if she left him. At home, she felt rejected by a stepfather and by her mother. Eventually she trusted me enough to seek me out individually. The involvement again, however, was built on the trust and discussion which had occurred in a group.

Furthermore, the more deeply and intensely one discusses human problems, the more one realizes that what may help one person may seem to actually hurt another. For example, teenagers should rightly be warned of the dangers involved in using LSD. This involves some element of fright. But if someone is involved in taking acid and is in a highly suggestible state, fear may be dangerous since it can precipitate a flashback.

The problem of hurting and helping at the same time could be further illustrated in other ways about other problems. Discussing an emotional problem in general may reassure some students of their normalcy and precipitate anxiety in others. For example, once a young person asked me the meaning of the term *manic-depressive*. She had heard the term and was concerned about her moodiness. When I explained that the term refers to a very extreme up and down cycle, she was relieved. But another teenager became afraid that her own moodiness could be termed manic-depressive. It took some persuasion on my part to convince her that mental illness is a matter of degree not kind, and that although her moods may fluctuate more than some people's, that does not make her or most people manic-depressive.

Because with increased involvement discussions often become more intense and may touch off more sensitive problems, it is important to keep the discussions at a safe level unless one is doing real therapy with a properly trained individual in charge.

Open Discussion

Many teenagers are not anxious to riot or break rules but want to be heard and, in turn, to hear other sides of various problems which confront them. When a problem arises in a school, a church or a society, it is often too late to establish a framework for open discussion. This kind of discussion does not come about overnight. Students and counselors alike need practice in developing the skills involved as well as the trust which is essential.

The use of circle discussions with the counselor acting as a participant rather than a dominant authority figure will free the discussions from formality. While the counselor must allow the discussion to flow rather freely, he should not be afraid to interject an opinion when that is warranted. However, it is better if he can direct the discussion so that the teenagers will arrive at their conclusions by themselves.

For example, in some of the discussions we have had in schools on handling angry feelings, the students have been able to arrive at sensible, constructive conclusions. At times I have used the approach of setting up hypothetical situations: "A teacher has just accused you of cheating (you haven't) and has insulted you by telling you that you could never have made such a high grade on your own. Now, what do you feel?"

Granted it is easier to force our opinions on young people than to guide them into the formation of their own conclusions, but the kind of person we will produce by our authoritarianism will be a credit to no one. It takes skill and practice to ask the right questions leading people to responsible answers, but skills can be developed, partly by trial and error. When one question does not generate discussion, try another until one "takes" and brings out some genuine, constructive responses. Open discussion through the use of group counseling is a tool we cannot afford to ignore nor delay using.

A fourteen-year-old girl who feels the aloneness of a school, church and whole society where she is not free to express her feelings or ask her questions wrote a plea for help—help which could be at least partly achieved through the closeness of a group:

> I am fourteen,
>   I am small.
> To look at this world
>   So large and tall,
> Frightens me with
>   A dreading fear
> Of people taking from me
>   All that is dear.
> Watching the world
>   With people always rushing,
> To a small person like me
>   Seems so crushing.
> I'm frightened. . . .

Group Interaction in the Home

Group interaction should not be thought of in only a formal setting. Thousands of times each day across this country young people gather informally in each other's homes. Obviously the parent cannot sit the teenager down and start a group discussion! However, many group discussions do start when young people meet casually together.

Some of the greatest learning experiences of my teen years grew out of a few of us stopping off at the home of a young couple after church. Many evenings we sat and ate vanilla ice cream with peaches on top and discussed everything from evolution to our own problems which we were facing at the time. The atmosphere permitted freedom of expression because no one denigrated us for what we said. We felt welcome but never pushed into discussion. The ice cream, the relaxed sitting on the floor, and the warmth in facial expressions as well as words made us feel we were accepted and could talk. Sometimes the couple invited us for dinner, at other times we baby-sat for them. We had a relationship with them and therefore the home was open for expression. Such could and should be true of many more Christian homes.

Group Fellowship in the Body of Christ

From a religious point of view research psychologist O. Hobart Mowrer makes the startling statement that "... an ideology which supremely stressed dedication to a larger power or order has deteriorated into a way of life which encourages or at least condones deep personal estrangement and alienation. Said more concisely, we have lost the strong sense of community and commitment which characterized early Christianity and have become disastrously individualistic, independent, and isolated."[5]

Similarly, according to Dr. Harvey Cox of Harvard Divinity School, "The earliest gathering of the followers of Jesus . . . lacked the cultic solemnity of most contemporary worship. These Christians gathered together for what they called the breaking of bread—that is, the sharing of a common meal. They had bread and wine, recalled the words of Jesus, read letters from the Apostles and other groups of Christians, exchanged ideas, sang, and prayed. Their worship services were rather uproarious affairs . . . more like the victory celebrations of a football team than what we usually call worship today."[6]

Such early gatherings of Christians provided for them what may come from church-oriented contemporary rap sessions with teenagers—a spiritual fellowship centered around the person of Jesus Christ.

When Paul speaks of the church as the body of Christ, he says, "The body has many parts, not just one part. If the foot says, 'I am not a part of the body because I am not a hand,' that does not make it any less a part of the body.... The eye can never say to the hand, 'I don't need you.' The head can't say to the feet, 'I don't need you.'" And "If one part suffers, all parts suffer with it, and if one part is honored, all the parts are glad. Now here is what I am trying to say: All of you together are the one body of Christ and each one of you is a separate and necessary part of it."[7] And in few situations can this mutual support and functioning of the body of Christ be seen better than in group discussions where the various members help and support each other.

Nor is such a technique merely part of a twentieth-century fad or an outgrowth of far-out encounter groups involving nudity and extreme sensitivity techniques. The concept of real group involvement is at least two thousand years old with roots deeply entrenched in the Christian church.

If the organized church, or any institution in our society, is to reach people through the use of groups, that church or school must be willing to step out and try an approach which is old—but new to the church today. It must be flexible, open to change and ready for criticism, for rarely does one become innovative without criticism.

Matthew Arnold wrote in "The Buried Life" the following lines which still express the fear and desire which are common to all men, young and old alike:

137

I knew the mass of men concealed
Their thoughts, for fear that if revealed
They would by other men be met
With blank indifference,
   or with blame reproved;

I knew they lived and moved
Tricked in disguises, alien to the rest
Of men, and alien to themselves—and yet
The same heart beats in every human breast!

Perhaps in these lines of Arnold's we find the most succinct argument for man's need to relate to other men without fear—to know that when he is really known, he will still be loved.

In Summary

1. We live in an era of alienation from God and from other people. There is a great need for the acceptance and closeness which can be achieved in caring groups.

2. Groups which help teenagers can be formal therapy groups, church groups, clubs or informal meetings in homes—each situation with a caring adult guide.

3. Groups help teenagers discover that others too have similar problems. These support and caring groups can also raise a member's self-esteem that results from knowing the acceptance and caring which people can give them.

4. While groups must encourage honestly, it is vital that the adult leadership be capable, not over-powering, and yet protective of feelings within the group.

5. Caring groups are not new. They are biblical—as begun by the early church—wherever Christians help, accept and encourage each other.

chapter seven

Communicating Christ's Love to Young People

There was a knock at the front door. As I opened it, I saw Shelley standing there. "Thank God you're here!" she said. Then came a burst of tears and near hysteria.

At that point all I could understand about Shelley was that she felt utterly worthless. Worthless enough that she no longer was sure she wanted to live. Brought up in a family which had emphasized her bad points and forced a ritualistic religious pattern at her, she had learned early to hate herself and to doubt that God could really care about her.

Now the self-hate came out into the open. A hate which sometime in the past had been covered by a mask of defensiveness wherein she had tried to prove her worth to others. Sometimes she had tried to buy love by purchasing gifts or doing favors. At other times she had protected herself by not getting close enough to anyone to really get hurt.

But now a series of rejections from family and friends

had brought her self-hate to the surface, and it was painful. She kept saying things like: "I hate myself—and my family. . . . I've got to have help or I'll never make it . . . please help me."

Then, as we continued to talk, she began to express her view that life itself was pretty worthless. Why were we born to start with? What was anyone's life really worth?

Her religious upbringing had been one of rules and little else. God had been made to seem distant and threatening. Churchgoing was associated with boredom and forced attendance. In contrast to what she was saying, the lines of an old hymn kept going through my mind:

> For the love of God is broader
> than the measures of man's mind
> and the heart of the Eternal
> is most wonderfully kind.
>
> But we make his love too narrow
> by false limits of our own
> and we magnify its strictness
> with a zeal He will not own.

Now as I tried to cut across that "strictness" to show her the love of God, I felt hedged in by all her background. I had to communicate across all the man-made religiosity and show her that God cared about her, was willing to accept her and could give her a life that was worth living.

Showing the Love of God
Yet sometimes the organized religious world makes it difficult for young people to see the love of God.

Susan was a pretty, eighteen-year-old girl who was very much alone in the world. Her starting salary at a dress shop was good, but not good enough to pay for an apartment, food and psychological help, too. Yet she needed and wanted to get competent help in solving problems which have deep roots in her personality.

The therapist she chose was one of the best and reasonably expensive. Yet because he was so well qualified, therapy with him could have turned out to be cheaper than a longer term of treatment with someone else.

The problem was money. One evening we sat down and figured out all of her expenses and income. The result was more encouraging than we had anticipated. If she did not do much but eat, work and sleep, she only needed twenty-five dollars more a month.

With considerable enthusiasm, we decided to look for a part-time job for her. Two days later I learned of a secretarial job in a local church. The hours were good. Pay was acceptable. And it was the perfect chance to get Susan involved in a church where Christ was presented. There she could experience real Christian love.

Susan called. A woman with a cold, efficient voice said, "I'm sorry I put that ad in the paper right now. I'm too busy to answer the phone."

Figuring it must have been just a bad day for her, Susan asked about the job. Yes, she said, she would hire Susan, but only to try her out. She didn't like someone young. She had had a bad experience before with a teenager.

The following week, Susan appeared at the church and worked hard. She got along well with the other, older volunteers and liked the work. But the lady remained aloof. At the end of the morning, she told Susan that she would try out other people and let her know in several weeks.

Susan had neither the reward of a permanent job offer nor the courtesy of a definite turn down. She was neither commended nor corrected. And the lady never called back.

A few weeks later, Susan found the kind of love I had hoped she would find in the church. Needing immediate medical care for a broken arm and not having the money to pay for it, she went to a local clinic that treats people who cannot afford to pay. It is located in an area heavily populated by young hippies, homosexuals and runaways. Many of the best doctors in the Los Angeles area donate time. Accountants, secretaries and people from other walks of life volunteer as nurses to help the doctors.

No one in the clinic preached Christ. No one claimed to have had his life transformed by the love of God. But that night they showed love to a lonely teenager who had not found it in church a few weeks before. As she put it, they showed her respect.

Today it seems the whole world is talking about love, probably because everyone needs it and so many cannot find it. In some cases real acts of kindness are being performed to back up the talk. But the emphasis of the Scripture is stronger. "All the special gifts and powers from God will someday come to an end, but love goes on forever."[1]

Loving with No Strings

In whatever capacity we find ourselves working with teenagers we must place trust in them if we expect to help them develop self-esteem, for our trust shows them that they are worth trusting. Love expects the best, and when once in a while that expectation is disappointed, love does not generalize and conclude that "All teens can't be trusted."

A teenage girl gives an example of the reverse of this quality of love: "Simple things are made to look awful. Like one time a couple I know was walking through a cemetery looking for tombstones with old dates. Pretty soon the girl got tired of walking and sat down under a tree. Her boyfriend sat down next to her and kissed her. So, what's wrong with that? But the caretaker happened to be walking by at the moment and what he saw was two more of those teenagers who had no morals, no sense of right and wrong." But real love trusts.

Real love is not happy when it can put someone down. In reference to the church, one boy says, "They really put them down if they're not really straight. I think that is really stupid. Like if someone is hooked, they don't try to help them. They think all teenagers are the same —rotten." And again, "The adults are too busy saving souls, they wouldn't become friends with the kids."

Yet what better way to "save souls" than to become friends? If we would be friends, we must be friends with no strings attached. Love has no ulterior motives.

One of the teenagers I have cared the most about and in whom I have invested much time and concern still drinks too much but not as much as before. Judy is still not a Christian. She is still not taking advantage of the psychological help which could be available. But she is better by far than she was a year ago and she is trying hard in her own, sometimes ineffective way.

I think she will make it someday. Someday she may be a person through whom Christ will operate in a unique way. And until then those of us who know her are not going to give up.

Yet blocking our efforts is another Christian with whom she had close contact. While this person thought Judy would become a Christian, she stuck with her tirelessly and tried to help. But after a while, when Judy had not become a Christian, the "friend" told her she was no longer interested in pursuing their friendship.

Love perseveres. It is easier to love when you can count the number of conversions you have each week or month or the number of people who have responded favorably to your counsel. But human love tends to give up when the object of that love does not respond quickly enough, when nothing seems to happen. Divine love never gives up. And that not giving up will lead to results in the long run partly because it shows that we really do care.

Not giving up means that the person you are involved with is important—and that you believe that eventually he will make it. It is therefore vital in any helping relationship that the person feels sure the counselor is going to stay with him until his problems are resolved. In some ways, such a commitment on the part of the counselor is the ultimate of caring.

Perseverance and continuity in caring are vital no matter what kind of problems the counselor is dealing with, for in no realm—spiritual, psychological or physical—can we expect immediate results. People often change slowly. And we must stay with them while they change.

Understanding Christian Growth

Even though Christ is more real than any acid trip because an acid trip is gone when you come down, yet there is a danger in thrill-seeking whether through a chemical or through God.

Our emotions are not geared to remain static. We feel it in our own lives. Our emotions change constantly. But occasionally a young person who has really found reality in Christ will become discouraged or even feel guilt when the original thrill leaves or subsides for a period.

144

In our eagerness to lead people to Christ, we are sometimes responsible for this disappointment because we promise sudden, complete transformation with no future problems, whereas in actuality Christian growth is a process on a day-by-day level.

A girl I recently met offered a good example of this. She explained, "I've been a Christian now for about four months. Before that I believed that life was just a trip. Do what you like, just as long as you don't hurt anyone. But really it was just a bummer. But like Jesus really blew my head. He said to me that my life is in Him. I'm living for Him. I should do everything to glorify Him. He really changed my Life. He gave me things I needed —wow, it was really far out. He gave me an awareness of people around me. See, it was really cool and it was a two-way process. You know, it seemed like the more I gave to Him or other people He would give me more back. I was really high on Jesus and He showed me that I must be rooted in Him."

She went on to explain her efforts to communicate Christ to her friends. And then the result: "Seeing people who were my friends turn me away really hurt me. I was left lonely, really lonely. I know Jesus wants me to fill my loneliness up with Him, but I need someone, you know, someone to share with, to cry to, to really have trust in. I need someone to talk to so badly. In order to regain my acceptance I began to talk like I was still doping. I wasn't though. Then I began to start but not in the beginning this time. I went straight to acid and speed. I tried not to let anyone know but I'm being found out. I know that Jesus should be my life, but I fight it. I don't even know who I am. I'm asking for help, I guess."

The Christian who originally showed her the life she could have in Christ, as well as any other Christian who now knows her, should be available to help. This is a prime function of the local church.

Yet too often the church functions more as a voice of politics or social comment or even of criticism than as an expression of the love of God.

Ignoring Unimportant Externals

Human love can bandage wounds and give a sense of worth to an individual. But in Christ we have access to a divine love which transcends anything human. He was practical in His love. He healed, fed the hungry, comforted those in sorrow, picked up the fallen.

Yet these smaller acts of kindness were not the greatest evidence of His love. He told his disciples, "This is my commandment: love one another, just as I love you. The greatest love a man can have for his friends is to give his life for them."[2]

This is the love of God to us. The ultimate of love. A love which led the God of the universe to give His only Son as a sacrifice for a race of human beings which rejected Him, spit on Him and put Him to death. Still He loved.

Humanly this quality of love is impossible. But according to the Bible, when we accept the sacrifice of Christ for our sin and commit our lives to Him, we become new—new people with a new love to communicate to the world.

Now is when people are grasping for love. Now is when we can communicate to them a love which will be beyond their expectation.

Yet the unfortunate fact is that we often communicate the very opposite of love. And as a result, we are unable to become involved with young people.

One young person whom I have recently met shows the scars of a religion which has not been centered in

Christ, in the embodiment of divine love, but in inconsistent rules—and resistance to change. Chuck is a sensitive person with strong beliefs. To him, Christ is a living reality. Yet his father warns his younger brother and sister not to turn out like Chuck. Why? Because Chuck's ideas on issues like dancing do not coincide with those of his father.

Chuck's parents have long lists of things they can and cannot do. They read the Bible daily and pray fervently and are always "rejoicing" in their relationship with God. Yet they fail to recognize the worth of a boy most parents would be proud of. They are inundated by an external value system which apparently keeps them from loving their own son.

Chuck finally asked to come in to talk. He wanted to know how to make his father respect him.

Many young people have been excluded from churches and schools because of a dress code which was unimportant in the first place and was dropped a few months later anyway. I have known clean cut, short-haired students who were deep into the drug scene. Others who dress differently may be living a pretty straight life. The language, music, dress of today's young person may not appeal to the adult world—nor does our life-style appeal to them. But if we are to reach across to each other, we must accept each other in these outward, unimportant ways and get to know each other where we are and for what we are.

Certainly this concept is scriptural. God says concerning the people's handsome choice for king: "Look not on his countenance, or on the height of his stature; because I have refused him: for the Lord seeth not as man seeth; for man looketh on the outward appearance, but the Lord looketh on the heart."[3]

So many externals that we seem to place much value

147

on, such as social status and outward appearance, are not the important things at all.

It is true that certain moral issues must be considered absolute. The Bible teaches that adultery is wrong in the sixteenth century or in the twentieth. So are gossip, slander, lying, murder and so on. But issues that are relative, such as a beard, the length of one's sideburns or drinking wine with one's dinner, should not be used as a stumbling block to a young person.

No young peson should be made to feel that coming to Christ is in essence a signing away of much of one's earthly pleasure and fun. Coming to Christ is much more profound than that. The major issue is commitment to Christ—not a lot of externals over which Christians themselves argue. It involves the commitment of all that I am to the authority of Christ. And once I am under His authority He will guide me in the formation of Christian ethics.

C.S. Lewis, perhaps more than any other contemporary writer, points out a balanced view on Christian ethics. In *Mere Christianity* he says: "While the rule of chastity is the same for all Christians at all times, the [social] rule of propriety changes. A girl in the Pacific islands wearing hardly any clothes and a Victorian lady completely covered in clothes might both be equally 'modest,' proper, or decent, according to the standards of their own societies: and both, for all we could tell by their dress, might be equally chaste (or equally unchaste)."[4]

Dr. Lewis continues: "I think that old, or old-fashioned, people should be very careful not to assume that young or 'emancipated' people are corrupt whenever they are (by the old standard) improper; and, in return, that young people should not call their elders prudes or Puritans because they do not easily adopt the new standard. A real desire to believe all the good you can of others and to make others as comfortable as you can will solve most of the problems."[5]

One needs only to look at the life of Christ to understand these words by the apostle Paul: "When with the heathen I agree with them as much as I can, except of course that I must always do what is right as a Christian. And so, by agreeing, I can win their confidence and help them too. . . . Yes, whatever a person is like, I try to find common ground with him so that he will let me tell him of Christ."[6]

As Christ walked this earth, He was upright and pure as no man had ever been before Him. John the Baptist said of Him, "I am not good enough even to untie his sandals."[7] Yet He was criticized by the religious world for eating with sinners and healing ("working") on the Sabbath.

We have no reason to believe that He wore shorter or longer hair than was the custom of His day. Nor were His garments conspicuously different. He paid taxes to Caesar. And He changed water to wine at a wedding. Somehow, if He were once again a man walking on this earth, I doubt that He would be majoring in debates over sideburns, beards and pantsuits. Or long hair and skirt lengths.

It is time that we who know Jesus Christ in a way which is so real we wish to communicate Him to others stop building roadblocks between Him and those we would reach.

Christ once said, "As for these little ones who believe in me—it would be better for a man to have a large millstone tied around his neck and be drowned in the deep sea, than for him to cause one of them to turn away from me. How terrible for the world that there are things that make people turn away! Such things will always happen—but how terrible for the one who causes them!"[8]

Facing the Challenge of Change

The church *needs* to change in order to fit the world in which it moves. Again, change need not imply compromise. Christ never compromised. When the money changers defiled the temple, He angrily chased them out. He forgave the adulteress but also told her to sin no more. Compromise is as phony as rigid rules and is not respected by teenagers or anyone else.

Once we forget about unimportant externals, we must still learn to come out of our own set way of thinking enough to understand what young people are really feeling—even when their feelings are foreign to us. They must be taken seriously if we are to have any form of communication with the younger generation.

Thus one of the biggest challenges that parents, teachers and pastors, as well as adults in general, face today is the challenge of change. Changes in thinking. Changes in methods. Changes in an entire life-style. Can we adjust to new methods and new thinking and yet preserve the truth and good of the old? Can we change?

Even in small details, we tend to be fixed into a position which is resistant to change. In a neighboring school, a teacher friend of mine had an experience which illustrates this point. One day he and his students were painting on a project when one of the students spilled some paint on his clothes. Needing some hot water immediately, my friend Joe took the student to the faculty washroom (student washrooms provide only cold water). There were several teachers in the faculty lounge, but Joe did not pay much attention to them since he and the student were in the washroom only a few minutes. The next day, Joe found the following note in his box, signed by one of those teachers:

"Yesterday when you brought a student into the faculty lounge, I could scarcely believe my eyes. Up to now I firmly believed that the faculty lounge was one place where we could at last be free from students. Now I know I was wrong. Please never let such a thing happen again."

Change from the ordinary pattern or routine, even for good reasons, seems to threaten many people. The inconsistency that results is seen in the school counselor who tells a counselee that she may talk only to him about her problems and not to a classroom teacher who has also taken an interest. It is visible in a curriculum which forces students through endless academic courses when their talent and interests lie in fine arts or trades. It is deeply entrenched in a social system which still segregates a black man in times of peace but allows him to die with a white man in times of war. It is evident in a job which pays a higher salary to a man than to a woman for the same skills.

Such rigid adherence to rules and old ways blocks creativity and stifles open solutions of individual problems in a school, church or society. Furthermore, in a church, it turns people away from seeing God for all that He really is.

A teenage couple have a two-year-old baby and move socially with doper friends. Bill's father is a successful businessman and Sue's parents attend a fundamentalist church. But Bill and Sue have turned away from their WASP background and find their entertainment in being loaded at parties. Pathetically enough, in addition to taking drugs themselves, these young parents also feed the baby marijuana. Confused, he hides in the corner or runs into a wall and doesn't feel the pain in his drug-dazed condition.

Yet just a few blocks away a moderately-sized church refused to provide professional counseling services because "it would set a precedent" and involve "unlocking washrooms." What they are really saying is "We don't want counseling in our church because we already give people the answer. If they don't take that, we don't want them." Yet all around them, other more liberal churches are providing trained counselors for people who have psychological problems.

Focusing on the Reality of Christ

We will never ultimately lead people to Jesus Christ by merely shedding our Puritan hang-ups. It seems to be an adult misconception that somehow we have to adjust our own values and lure teenagers into the church with some cheap bait.

Amy Carmichael in her pamphlet *God's Missionary* states the issue well: "Can we reach them by being as like them as possible (only possibly a little more decorously dull)? Is that the line of power? We hold that it is not. How then are these to be won? *The Cross is the attraction.*"[9]

Jesus Christ is attractive enough without our gimmicks and tricks. If we would merely reflect Him to others without roadblocks and man-made laws, many would cease to resist Him as the answer to their problems.

How do we make them listen to us? We do not make them. We accept them. We care. We listen. We do not compromise, for to do so would be to lose respect. But we respect their differences as we expect them to respect ours. And then, in an atmosphere of love, we allow Christ to become the real issue. We introduce them to Him. And He will do the rest, for He is still a seeking God. In the words of another old hymn:

I sought the Lord,
  and afterward I knew
He moved my heart
  to seek Him, seeking me:
It was not I that found,
  O Saviour true;
No, I was found of Thee.

A church which is changing and growing will be a usable vehicle for a seeking God to reach men and women of all ages. And in a strange way, the organized church will not be the center of attraction, but rather the focus will be on God Himself. And to the reality of Jesus Christ most young people are receptive.

Not long ago a fifteen-year-old girl sat across from me, asking me to stop her from taking her own life. On her wrists were deep gashes and scars from where she had cut herself before. Across the top of her arm were scars from other self-inflicted injuries. When I asked her if her parents cared, she said, "I suppose so; they had me. But they never tell me they care so it's as if they really don't."

Then I asked her if she had ever asked God to help her. In her reply she described the church she had attended—narrow, closed up into itself, status-conscious, full of cliques, unloving. So she gave up and wrote of her despair in the following poem:

I am your lost sheep Lord
Yet when you seek me you do not look
I am the house built on the Rock
which could not comprehend
  the might of the hurricane.
I am the seed sowed in the rich brown earth
  who knew not the meaning of drought

I am the peasant who gave her last coin
   to the service of the Lord
Yet received no joyous heart,
   only an empty belly
I am lost.

Bridging the Generation Gap

Those of us who function within the Christian world, and out from that world to others who do not share our commitment to Christ, vary in our degree of training and innate, intuitive sensitivity to the needs of others. We have different backgrounds and different gifts from God. Yet each one of us has a God-given responsibility to care about the next person, whether that person is a conservatively-oriented churchgoer or a long-haired, pot-smoking hippie. Only our pride will stop us from caring about people who are different from us—twisted pride which makes us somehow feel superior. But we have only to read the Scriptures to find out that God condemns spiritual pride above all other sins.

Dr. Karl Menninger has written, "When a trout rising to a fly gets hooked on a line and finds himself unable to swim about freely, he begins with a fight which results in struggles and splashes and sometimes an escape. Often, of course, the situation is too tough for him. In the same way the human being struggles with his environment and with the hooks that catch him. Sometimes he masters his difficulties; sometimes they are too much for him. His struggles are all that the world sees and it naturally misunderstands them. It is hard for a free fish to understand what is happening to a hooked one."

To care, to be sensitive to the varying needs of those whom we encounter, to understand what we may not have experienced ourselves: These qualities we must possess if we are to begin to bridge the so-called generation gap, which exists not only between teenagers and adults but between any two individuals who are incapable of trusting and understanding each other.

Finally, if we are to help another person, we must learn to see beyond the problems which trouble him to the potential which exists within him. In the words of Goethe, "If we treat people as they are, we make them worse. If we treat them as if they were what they ought to be, we help them to become what they are capable of becoming."

To help a person become what he is capable of becoming—that is the goal of the counseling process.

In Summary

1. If teenagers are to receive help they must feel unconditional love, a love which extends beyond a list of legalistic rules.

2. The church's obligation is to offer all of its members something far greater than social life, essential as that is; for even the very young have an inner, God-given longing to know God. They need to know they can be related to Him through Jesus Christ.

3. The primary goal for helping anyone can be summed up in the concluding words of this book: "To help a person become what he is capable of becoming" by God's grace.

Footnotes

Chapter One
1. Walter Lippmann, quoted in *The Pursuit of Meaning* by Joseph B. Fabry (Boston: Beacon Press, 1968), p. 101.
2. Ibid.

Chapter Two
1. Fabry, p. 29.
2. J. Thomas Ungerleider, M.D., ed., *The Problems and Prospects of LSD* (Springfield, Ill.: Charles C. Thomas, 1968), pp. 66–67.
3. Jeremiah 29:11 (Rotherham).

Chapter Three
1. Charles H. Spurgeon, "Discouragement," HIS, 22 (February 1962), p. 9.
2. Martyn Lloyd-Jones, *Spiritual Depression: Its Causes and Cure* (Grand Rapids: Eerdmans, 1965), pp. 18–19.
3. Kenneth Wuest, *Word Studies: The Greek New Testament for the English Readers* (Grand Rapids: Eerdmans, 1955), p. 211.
4. Romans 3:23 (RSV).
5. Mark 12:31 (RSV).
6. Rollo May, *Man's Search for Himself* (New York: W.W. Norton & Co., 1953), p. 100.
7. C.S. Lewis, *Mere Christianity* (New York: Macmillan, 1960), pp. 84–85.
8. 1 John 1:9 (RSV).
9. Ephesians 4:26 (KJV).
10. Viktor E. Frankl, *Man's Search for Meaning* (New York: Washington Square Press, 1963), p. 172.
11. "The major symptoms an autistic child displays are self-destructive binges in which the child bashes his head against walls or chews on his own fingers; total emotional withdrawal from people and life; and unabating preoccupation with sameness—estab-

lished routines must be followed exactly; the slightest deviation can trigger an outburst of violence." Tod Faulkner, "Autism: Still More Questions and Answers," *West Magazine* in *Los Angeles Times,* (9 April 1972), p. 26.

Chapter Four

1. William Glasser, *Reality Therapy* (New York: Harper & Row, 1965), p. 12.
2. Ibid., p. 7.
3. Morris Rosenberg, *Society and the Adolescent Self Image* (Princeton: University Press, 1965), pp. 144–45.
4. *Los Angeles Herald Examiner,* 22 November 1970, p. A-7, col. 3.
5. Mark 2:17 (Good News for Modern Man).
6. John 14:18 (Living Bible).
7. Matthew 28:20 (Living Bible).
8. Genesis 2:18 (NASB).
9. 2 Timothy 1:16–18 (TEV).
10. Mark 14:34, 37 (NASB).
11. Frankl, quoted in Fabry, p. 63.
12. Rollo May, *The Art of Counseling* (Nashville: Abingdon Press, 1967), p. 170.
13. Mark 6:31 (Living Bible).
14. John 4:53 (KJV).

Chapter Five

1. May, *The Art of Counseling,* p. 77.
2. Romans 12:15 (Living Bible).
3. 2 Corinthians 2:3 (TEV).
4. May, *The Art of Counseling,* p. 119.
5. Psalm 139:14 (KJV).
6. May, *The Art of Counseling,* p. 162.

Chapter Six

1. Alvin Toffler, *Future Shock* (New York: Bantam Books, 1970), p. 97.
2. Ibid., p. 122.
3. Quoted in Toffler, p. 341.
4. O. Hobart Mowrer, *The New Group Therapy* (New York: Van Nostrand Reinhold, 1964), p. 89.
5. Ibid., p. 24.
6. Harvey Cox, "*Worship:* Clock or Celebration—an Interview with Harvey Cox," *Colloquy,* I (February 1968).
7. 1 Corinthians 12:14–15, 21, 26–27 (Living Bible).

Chapter Seven

1. 1 Corinthians 13:8 (Living Bible).
2. John 15:12–13 (TEV).
3. 1 Samuel 16:7 (KJV).
4. C.S. Lewis, p. 88.
5. Ibid., p. 89.
6. 1 Corinthians 9:21–22 (Living Bible).
7. John 1:27 (TEV).
8. Matthew 18:6–7 (TEV).
9. Amy Carmichael, *God's Missionary* (Fort Washington, Pa.: Christian Literature Crusade, 1939), p. 28.

Bibliography

Carmichael, Amy. *God's Missionary.* Fort Washington, Pa.: Christian Literature Crusade, 1939.

Cox, Harvey. *Colloquy* I. February, 1968.

Frankl, Viktor E. *Man's Search for Meaning.* New York: Washington Square Press, 1963.

Glasser, William. *Reality Therapy.* New York: Harper & Row, 1965.

Lloyd-Jones, Martyn. *Spiritual Depression: Its Causes and Cure.* Grand Rapids: Eerdmans, 1965.

Lewis, C.S. *Mere Christianity.* New York: Macmillan, 1960.

Lippmann, Walter. Quoted in *The Pursuit of Meaning* by Joseph B. Fabry. Boston: Beacon Press, 1968.

————. *Los Angeles Herald Examiner*, 22 November 1970, p. A-7.

May, Rollo. *Man's Search for Himself.* New York: W.W. Norton & Co., 1953.

May, Rollo. *The Art of Counseling.* Nashville: Abingdon Press, 1967.

Mowrer, O. Hobart. *The New Group Therapy.* New York: Van Nostrand Reinhold, 1964.

Rosenberg, Morris. *Society and the Adolescent Self Image.* Princeton: University Press, 1965.

Spurgeon, Charles H. "Discouragement," HIS, 22 February, 1962.

Toffler, Alvin, *Future Shock.* New York: Bantam Books, 1970.

Ungerleider, J. Thomas, M.D. ed., *The Problems and Prospects of LSD.* Springfield, Il.: Charles C. Thomas, 1968.

Wuest, Kenneth. *Word Studies: The Greek New Testament for the English Readers.* Grand Rapids: Eerdmans, 1955.